Our Food, Our Right

Recipes for Food Justice

published by the **Community Alliance for Global Justice**

Our Food, Our Right

Recipes for Food Justice

Second Edition

Foreword by
Raj Patel

Seattle, 2012

Our Food, Our Right: Recipes for Food Justice
Second Edition
A Publication of the Food Justice Project, CAGJ
Entire work copyright © CAGJ 2012, with copyright to each work—essays, articles and
recipes—held by the various authors. Permissions for reproduction of any kind must be
obtained from each individual author, and can be requested through the CAGJ office.

Cover illustration copyright © Nikki McClure
Cover photograph copyright © David W. Lynch

Art direction & cover design by Annie Brulé
Book design by Annie Brulé & Phil Bevis

Photos/Illustrations inside the book are credited adjacent to the graphic, with the exception
of those images in the public domain and without copyright, which are not credited. Crows
that appear in the margins, denoting relevant side notes, are copyright Nikki McClure and
used with permission. Line art throughout is by Pearson Scott Foresman [Public domain],
via Wikimedia Commons. Engravings throughout are by Dover [public domain].

*We invite you to enjoy the first edition of "Our Food, Our Right: Recipes for Food Justice"!
It is a 72-page zine. With the exception of the DIY food-preserving section, all material is
different from the second edition. CAGJ sells it on a sliding scale, $5–$20, and you can order
from our website: www.seattleglobaljustice.org/cagjstore*

Paperback ISBN: 978-0985342029

Printed on minimum 30% recycled FSC-certified paper by Thomson-Shore, a 100%
worker-owned manufacturer of hard and softcover books.

Published by CAGJ: Community Alliance for Global Justice
606 Maynard Ave. S. #102 Seattle, WA 98104
Seattle, Washington
(206) 405-4600
www.seattleglobaljustice.org

Thank You to Our Generous Partners & Sponsors!

BOOK SPONSORS

People's Memorial Funeral Co-op

Brulé Illustration & Design

People's UFCW Local 21

Arundel Books

Mary & Raymond Camezon	Judy Pigott	Steve Lansing & Bonnie Valiton
Naomi Kageyama	Janie Starr	

PROJECT PARTNERS

Central Co-op's Madison Market
Applied Research Center

Allan Paulson	Cheryl Houser	Maria Elena Rodriguez
Audrey & Pierre Day	David W. Lynch	Marina Skumanich
Burke Stansbury	Jacques-Jean Tiziou	Melodie Woods
Cindy Buhse & Rachael Brady	Jeff Makholm	Mercedes Ridao

COMMUNITY PARTNERS

Bottlehouse   Yes! Magazine

Aaron Wood	Jenna & Kate	Megan McBride
Alan & Amy Huggins	Jennifer Williams	Mia Devine
Barb and Dave	Judi Finney	Milissa Orzolek
Caroline Faria	Judy Sorrell	Nan Geer
Charlie Zarkadas & Maryellen Hassell	Kacy McKinney	Peter Blomquist
Chris Iberle	Kathy & Tom Iberle	Reverend Hunter Davis & David Godsey
David Banta & Caroline Coggeshall	Katie Apone	Rob Day
Dolores Lenore	Kristin Makholm	Sharon Lerman & Mike Graham-Squire
Eitan Isaacson	Lynne Barker	Teresa Mares
Elena Perez	Make Flaherty	Wendy Johnson
Ellen O'Shea	Mary Ann Schroeder	

...And to the dozens and dozens, too numerous to list, who gave everything from five to 45 dollars in support of this book. Heartfelt thanks to everyone who joined our Community Supported Publishing campaign! In the multifaceted fundraising environment, we may have missed some of your names, and we truly appreciate all your contributions that made this book possible. Any omitted names brought to our attention will be included in subsequent printings.

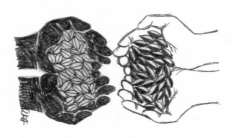

The second edition of "Our Food, Our Right: Recipes for Food Justice" is the result of a truly collective effort. CAGJ would like to thank the many people who have contributed articles, recipes, time, love, energy, passion, drawings, poems, advice, and more. As a community-based project, "Our Food, Our Right" was shaped primarily by the knowledge, skills and creativity that you shared with us. Each voice in this book is unique and meaningful. Each is an integral part of the story we are telling together, through words and through action, about a more just food system and a more just world.

A special thank you to the team of volunteers who guided CAGJ through the process of publishing both the 1st and 2nd editions of our book!

Second Edition Coordinators
Karla Makholm, Joanna Wright

Publication Coordinators: Annie Brulé & Phil Bevis

Organizing Committee: Katie Apone, Jaclyn Dagger, Victoria Gibson, Kayla Hornbrook, Cheryl Kleinman, Karla Makholm, Maria Rodriguez, Joanna Wright

Editorial team: Annie Brulé, Graham Clark, Karen Cowgill, Michelle Venetucci Harvey, Karla Makholm, Amanda Welch, Joanna Wright

Members of CAGJ and Food Justice Project Members:
Heather Day (Executive Director, CAGJ), Victoria Gibson, Chris Iberle, Karla Makholm, Teresa Mares, Maria Rodriguez, Laura Titzer, Joanna Wright

Thank you to the many people and community organizations whose work inspired this book. There are too many to list, and we honor your steadfast commitment in the struggle for food justice and food sovereignty for all people, everywhere.

drawing by Ashley Fent

Blessing Prayer

Bless the hands of the people of the earth,
The hands that plant the seed,
The hands that bind the harvest,
The hands that carry the burden of life.
Soften the hands of the oppressor and
Strengthen the hands of the oppressed.
Bless the hands of the workers,
Bless the hands of those in power above them
That the measure they deal will be tempered
With justice and compassion. Amen.

Oración de la Bendición

Bendice las manos de los pueblos de la tierra,
Las manos que plantan la semilla,
Las manos que juntan la cosecha,
Las manos que llevan la carga de la vida.
Suaviza las manos del opresor y
Fortalece las manos de los oprimidos.
Bendice las manos de los trabajadores,
Bendice las manos de aquellos con poder sobre ellos
De manera que la medida que dispensen esté templada
Por la justicia y la compasión. Amén.

Courtesy of National Farm Worker Ministry, a faith based organization that supports farm workers as they organize for justice and empowerment. www.nfwm.org

CONTENTS

10

Foreword
Raj Patel

I once read a rumor that the world's best food was to be found in Austria. The story goes like this: the fine Tyrolean local ingredients, the climate, the altitude, the cattle, the dairy, the garlic, the water, and the technique all come together to make an unforgettable culinary experience; sadly, the minute you try to cook Austrian food outside Austria, it tastes chewy and gamey and, frankly, a bit crap. That's why no one knows about it, and why there's little chance it'll catch on.

When it comes to social change, there aren't recipes. It's as impossible to replicate social change from one context to another as it is, allegedly, to cook good Austrian food outside Austria. That's as it should be. Everywhere, everyone, is different. What works in one place might fail in another. A visionary in one community can be a laughingstock outside. And even when social change succeeds, conservative forces learn and adapt. Look to the patterns of success and failure after the Arab Spring, to see this unfolding today.

So why a social change cookbook? Cooking is one of the few activities where we get to make mistakes, live with them, and learn from them. Cookbooks are guides, to help prevent things curdling, to suggest how things have worked before, and hint at surprising combinations of how they might work tonight. The joy of cooking isn't to follow the recipe, but to invent one's own and share what works and what doesn't.

That's why this cookbook is filled with recipes and evaluations, how to's and how not to's, and even stories about culinary academies—a how to put together a how-to. It's a cookbook with politics that can be as joyful as the food. For a publication like this to go into its second edition points to another feature of today's

food movement—that it is young, ready to experiment, and looking for lessons and inspiration.

But what you'll not find here is the whiff of self-satisfaction. Too often in the recent breathless celebration of the local food movement, the agenda has become parochial. You know the line: as long as I'm eating my homegrown heirloom tomatoes and chewy kale product, all's good. But this is a cookbook with a global vision. While food prices clearly hurt Americans—particularly households headed by single women—food inflation hurts people in the Global South a great deal more.

A great deal of harm is being done by development agencies and corporations in the Global South. In the Global North, especially in the United States, we bear a greater burden because a greater harm is being done in our name. With our dollars USAID, the Millennium Challenge Corporation and the World Bank are fomenting new food crises. Their investment in fossil fuel development is contributing to climate change—since 1980 by one estimate, commodity prices are 19% higher as a result of climate change. They deregulate financial markets, creating the space in which speculators can, through vehicles like the Goldman Sachs Commodity Index, make profit from hunger.

If we stand and watch this horror, we're complicit, and there's little self-satisfaction to be had from that. Getting active in order to fight the bigger problems in the global food system is hard—daunting even. If only there were some way that we could connect the global and the local, if only there were a reference guide that helped bring it all together with ideas for change, and perhaps with some good recipes.

You hold such a manual in your hands. Ideas from this second edition can help us understand our community and responsibilities better, and not feel overwhelmed by the task ahead. So let's get started. There are mistakes to be made and learned from. Garlic to be fried. Joy to be shared.

Introduction
by CAGJ's Food Justice Project

"Local Food" is making it big these days, and can be viewed as anything from a buzzword to a powerful movement. Whether someone is turned on to eating locally because of scares over food safety and food prices, concerns about the environment and climate change, supporting local economies, eating healthier, or simply having enough to eat and nourish a family, it's catching on. When Wal-Mart and McDonald's are at least paying lip-service to the idea, if not trying to co-opt the political and social movement, you know you're making an impact.

Eating locally isn't just about the exponentially expanding network of farmers' markets, getting your CSA box, growing some kale, and buying Fair Trade and organic. Those are certainly part of it, but "voting with your dollar" can only go so far when pitted against the conventional, corporate, industrial food system. For example, consider the large number of people who cannot afford these normally expensive items or the plight of conventional food workers and producers who are exploited in the food chain.

consumers cannot simply buy a better food system

And this is exactly the point. Consumers cannot simply buy a better food system. Only systemic, political, and social change brought about by diverse groups of people can build real alternatives to the broken way we produce and eat our food. How we grow and eat our food is too important an issue to keep in the hands of a few profit-driven decision makers who have enforced policies and practices that turn food into a commodity rather than treating it as a basic human need

13

and right with intimate ties to place and culture. We've seen the industrial agriculture model at work: deeply rooted in neoliberal economics, it drives down wages and prices and displaces farmers worldwide through NAFTAs, CAFTAs, and WTOs. This model means corporate consolidation and big agribusiness with profit as its sole purpose, feeding people unsafe, unhealthy food (and leaving many others hungry) in urban and rural areas, destroying the land, fostering inhumane conditions for workers and poverty-level wages that don't even provide workers with the resources to eat the food they work to produce, and trapping small and mid-sized farmers into a supply and distribution chain that pushes many off the land and gives incentives for larger and larger scale.

Monoculture dominates our food system, decreasing biodiversity of crops and breeds, and threatening ecological sustainability and farmers' livelihoods. Commodity crops, particularly in the Global North, receive high subsidies and support in spite of negative impacts on public health and local economies here and everywhere. All resources and inputs are treated as commodities to be exploited, down to the workers themselves. Industrial capitalist agriculture, from production to processing to distribution to consumption, simultaneously generates waste and hunger, profits and poverty around the world; such are the intense contradictions of a deeply broken global food system.

What are the impacts? Heavily dependent on fossil fuels, industrial agriculture contributes to climate change while undermining the biodiversity needed to build resilient food systems capable of adapting to drought, floods, and other shifting conditions. As fossil fuel resources are depleted, limitations on the source, quantity, affordability, and ecological stability of food and land will arise. The obesity crisis and other health epidemics are the externalized costs of corporate food that is offered in our schools and grocery stores, drowning out alternatives with sheer quantity, cheaper prices, and advertising. Racism, sexism, classism, and other oppressions run rampant, restricting access to food and productive resources (land, water, and seed) for women, people of color, and the poor in the United States and throughout the Global South. Subsistence farmers, who are primarily women, are pushed off the land and marginalized by industrial food.

Political and economic decisions made by the powerful on things like corporate mergers and acquisitions, undermining workers' rights, subsidies, trade agreements, purchasing policies, regulations, and labeling, preserve this model. Such top-down 'reforms' overwhelmingly serve to maintain the status quo while making its problems less visible and thereby minimizing resistance; business-as-usual can continue underneath a green-washed veneer, obscured from view by a growing niche market of farmers' markets, CSA programs, and even Certified Organic products.

So as we move forward and create the new food system—which the stories of change in the following pages illustrate—in the shell of the old food system, we must confront the powerful interests that will not give up without a fight. Food corporations and conglomerates, trade lobbyists, seed companies, chemical companies, oil companies, and even weapons manufacturers have a lot at stake. They must be confronted through legislation, political action, civil disobedience, public exposure, education, strikes, boycotts, flash mobs, community organizing, community gardens, guerrilla gardens, direct action, and whatever tools we can mobilize to challenge the power structure from the grassroots. Everyone has the right to eat and produce healthy, local, culturally and ecologically appropriate foods, and the global food sovereignty movement can make this a lasting reality. We need to come together in bold and creative ways to change our plates, our school cafeteria, our friend's cafeteria, our grocery store, our restaurants, the suppliers, the manufacturers, the farmers and producers, the companies, and the global economy to reflect the values we all share.

Everyone has the right to eat and produce healthy, local, culturally and ecologically appropriate foods

—the Food Justice Project team, Chris, Heather, Joanna, Karla, Laura, Maria, Teresa, and Victoria

A Note On the Origin & Organization of the 2nd Edition: Positive Stories of Change

The first edition of *Our Food, Our Right: Recipes for Food Justice*, explored a variety of issues about the food system, especially in regards to how it was broken—ecologically, economically, and socially. There has been a growing conversation in this country about why this system is not working for people or for the environment. The first edition of this book offered a spectrum of voices engaged in this conversation.

With the second edition, the *Our Food, Our Right* committee wanted to build upon this conversation by focusing specifically on positive stories of change. Our guiding questions were: How does our understanding of what is broken in the food system, especially in regards to systemic oppression and alienation of people from each other and from the land, inform the way we go about creating viable, just alternatives? What do these alternatives look like? What are some real examples of how people are moving away from the old paradigm of environmental and social exploitation, towards a food system that is healthier and more just, not only for individual consumers but also for farmers, food workers, and communities? We hope that these stories of change are informative, inspiring, and empowering.

Although the committee organized the articles in this book into "local" and "global" categories, we recognize that the local and the global are inherently interconnected. What happens at home, in our own bodies, at our dinner tables, in our neighborhoods and our stores, on local farmland, and in local watersheds, affects and is affected by people and ecosystems far beyond our borders. Nothing happens in isolation. Each of our actions have global impact.

Community Alliance for Global Justice

Who we are:

Community Alliance for Global Justice educates and mobilizes with individuals and organizations to strengthen local economies everywhere. CAGJ is grassroots, community-based and committed to anti-oppressive organizing as we build solidarity across diverse movements. CAGJ seeks to transform unjust trade and agricultural policies and practices imposed by corporations, governments and other institutions while creating and supporting alternatives that embody social justice, sustainability, diversity and grassroots democracy.

Food Justice Project

Food Justice is the right of communities everywhere to produce, distribute, access, and eat good food regardless of race, class, gender, ethnicity, citizenship, ability, religion, or community. Good food is healthful, local, sustainable, culturally appropriate, humane, and produced for the sustenance of people and the planet.

Through political action, anti-oppressive organizing and community-building, CAGJ's Food Justice Project seeks to challenge and transform the globalized, industrial, corporate-driven food system and promote existing alternatives as we join the global struggle for food sovereignty for all! Our Community Education focus includes Teach-Outs supporting and visiting local food sites, and publication of the *Our Food, Our Right* handbook.

AGRA Watch

AGRA Watch is a project of CAGJ that challenges the Gates Foundation's problematic agricultural development programs in Africa, including the Alliance for a Green Revolution in Africa (AGRA). We work in solidarity with African farmers, activists, and civil society organizations resisting land grabs, industrial agriculture, GMOs, and other undemocratic initiatives pushed from the outside at the expense of farmers, consumers, and the environment. AGRA Watch participates in national and international organizing efforts to build community-based, agroecological solutions to hunger and climate change here, in Africa, and around the world.

Trade Justice

CAGJ works for Trade Justice by organizing to reform the current US trade model that prioritizes profits over people and the environment, while offering viable alternatives through democratic engagement. Through CAGJ's Trade Action Network, and membership in the WA Fair Trade Coalition, CAGJ continues our historic organizing to halt future so-called Free Trade Agreements, including the pending Trans Pacific Partnership, and to monitor existing policy including NAFTA, CAFTA and bilateral agreements with Peru, Colombia, South Korea and Panama. We seek to increase public understanding of trade by educating and advocating about the links to our food system, food sovereignty, immigrant rights, climate justice and economic justice.

Northwest Farm Bill Action Group

Northwest Farm Bill Action Group (NWFBAG) is building a diverse alliance of people and organizations in the Pacific Northwest who advocate for a more healthy, sustainable, and equitable food system. Through collaboration, we provide a space for Pacific Northwest communities to educate themselves about the upcoming Farm Bill and to cultivate the tools to take action and effect policy change to work for a better food system. CAGJ launched NWFBAG in August 2010, and continues to play a leadership role in its activities.

What is Food Sovereignty?
CAGJ

Food sovereignty is the right of people to determine their own food and agricultural policies; essentially, the democratization of food and agriculture. Food sovereignty is a movement begun by farmers, fisherfolk, indigenous peoples, and landless workers. It is comprised of communities throughout the world that lack control of basic resources to sustain themselves—seeds, food, land, and water—as a result of top-down trade, development, and agricultural policies. The global movement for food sovereignty calls for countries, regions, and communities to regain control of their own resources in order to feed themselves.

La Via Campesina developed the concept of food sovereignty and brought it to public debate during the World Food Summit in 1996 as an alternative to neoliberal policies. Since then, the concept has become central to international debates about agriculture, even within United Nations bodies.

Food sovereignty is the right of people to determine their own food and agricultural policies; it is the democratization of food and agriculture.

In 2009 the Community Food Security Coalition awarded the Food Sovereignty Prize for the first time. CAGJ was honored to be awarded the Food Sovereignty Honorable Mention Prize, along with the Toronto Food Policy Council and the International Centre of Insect Physiology and Ecology, of Kenya. La Via Campesina, whose words appear on the next page, won the prize. The prize was awarded to "recognize organizations who have performed significant work to promote food sovereignty by raising public awareness, on-the-ground action, or developing and implementing programs and policies; and groups who recognize the importance of collective action in brining about social change; global linkages in food sovereignty work; and the importance of women in agriculture and food issues."

Seven Principles of Food Sovereignty
La Via Campesina

- *Food As a Basic Human Right*
- *Agrarian Reform*
- *Protecting Natural Resources*
- *Reorganizing Food Trade*
- *Ending the Globalization of Hunger*
- *Social Peace*
- *Democratic Control of Agricultural Policies*

1. Food As a Basic Human Right.

Everyone must have access to safe, nutritious and culturally appropriate food in sufficient quantity and quality to sustain a healthy life with full human dignity. Each nation should declare that access to food is a constitutional right and guarantee the development of the primary sector to ensure the concrete realization of this fundamental right.

2. Agrarian Reform.

A genuine agrarian reform is necessary which gives landless and farming people—especially women—ownership and control of the land they work and returns territories to indigenous peoples. The right to land must be free of discrimination on the basis of gender, religion, race, social class or ideology; the land belongs to those who work it.

3. Protecting Natural Resources.

Food Sovereignty entails the sustainable care and use of natural resources, especially land, water, and seeds and livestock breeds. The people who work the land must have the right to practice sustainable management of natural resources and to conserve biodiversity free of restrictive intellectual property rights. This can only be done from a sound economic basis with security of tenure, healthy soils and reduced use of agro-chemicals.

4. Reorganizing Food Trade.

Food is first and foremost a source of nutrition and only secondarily an item of trade. National agricultural policies must prioritize production for domestic consumption and food self-sufficiency. Food imports must not displace local production nor depress prices.

5. Ending the Globalization of Hunger.

Food Sovereignty is undermined by multilateral institutions and by speculative capital. The growing control of multinational corporations over agricultural policies has been facilitated by the economic policies of multilateral organizations such as the WTO, World Bank and the IMF. Regulation and taxation of speculative capital and a strictly enforced Code of Conduct for TNCs is therefore needed.

6. Social Peace.

Everyone has the right to be free from violence. *Food must not be used as a weapon.* Increasing levels of poverty and marginalization in the countryside, along with the growing oppression of ethnic minorities and indigenous populations, aggravate situations of injustice and hopelessness. The ongoing displacement, forced urbanization, increasing incidence of racism, and repression of smallholder farmers cannot be tolerated.

7. Democratic control.

Smallholder farmers must have direct input into formulating agricultural policies at all levels. The United Nations and related organizations will have to undergo a process of democratization to enable this to become a reality. Everyone has the right to honest, accurate information and open and democratic decision-making. These rights form the basis of good governance, accountability and equal participation in economic, political and social life, free from all forms of discrimination. Rural women, in particular, must be granted direct and active decision-making on food and rural issues.

Food Sovereignty is defined in many ways the world over.
Thanks to La Via Campesina for this definition of Food Sovereignty.
www.viacampesina.org

Terry Hope

The Farm Job

Why are you going to Virginia?
asked my grandfather.
I can find a farm for you to work on here in Indiana.

Why are you working on a farm?
That was the unasked question.

I didn't know how to answer him,
but just as I took my college education for granted,
never did he question the heft of a shovel,
or the sun on the back of his neck.

Gretchen Sneegas

Local Stories of Change
Positive Solutions *from* the Pacific Northwest
and Across the U.S.

The Color of Food

Applied Research Center

"The Color of Food" explores the universe of workers that populate the food chain. The full report, excerpted here and available through www.arc.org, is intended to support the collaborative efforts of advocates and researchers who are working diligently to bring attention to the invisible labor that drives the food supply chain.

Food justice seeks to ensure that the benefits and risks of where, what and how food is grown, produced, transported, distributed, accessed and eaten are shared fairly. Food justice represents a transformation of the current food system, including but not limited to eliminating disparities and inequities.[1]

In the United States, more than 20 million people are workers in the food chain,[2] over 11 million of whom are full-time employees earning an income.[3] Movements to make healthy food accessible to everyone are increasing in popularity, which is an important step towards achieving food equity for people of color. However, more attention must be paid to the often-invisible labor that produces and prepares the food that we put on the table.

The *good food movement* narrowly focuses on the relationship between the producer and consumer, and to the environmental benefits of sustainable agriculture.[4] Consumers strive to directly relate to the process of food production, getting to know the conditions under which their eggs or vegetables were raised. They purchase food directly from the farmer or grow the crops themselves, shortening the time and space between when the food is first planted as a seed and when it is eaten by the consumer.

1   Gottlieb, Robert, and Joshi, Anupama. Food Justice. The MIT Press, October 2010.
2   Based on analysis by the Data Center, using data from the Bureau of Labor Statistics, August 2010.
3   For the purposes of this report, we defined a food worker as someone who was employed in a food-related industry and earned a positive income in the past year.
4   Personal communication with Saru Jayaraman, Co-Director, Restaurant Opportunities Centers United. February 11, 2010.

The Good Food Movement

Contemporary food production, like much of our economy, is dominated by large corporations, and these corporations produce edibles through an industrial process.[5] The food chain is incorporated in the world capitalist system, where crops are grown in the global or domestic south, often in fields of monoculture crops, using bioengineered seeds and subjected to harsh pesticides; then the products are packaged and shipped to the end consumer.[6] What we see on the supermarket shelves or serve to eat is a food product, alienated from the natural and social world.

The good food movement—also known as *eco-food, slow food, real food, local food* or the *sustainable food movement*—is a reaction to the world food system. It's driven largely by the middle class, nostalgic for a pre-industrial mode of food production, who demand organic food grown locally by independent farmers. The roots of this tradition stem from Thomas Jefferson, who believed that a nation of small farmers would be morally virtuous, economically independent and the citizenry of an equitable republic.[7] However, Jefferson's vision ignored or glossed over the slave labor that powered agrarian economies, the history of colonization and the displacement of people of color from their land.[8]

The overarching desire is for a sustainable food system—sustainable for the earth, consumers, and family farmers. Consumers vote with their purchases, favoring produce sold in a farmer's market over a chain supermarket, supporting an urban farm in a community of color by subscribing to a monthly box of vegetables and fruits, or redistributing fruit foraged from backyards to the community.

5   *Francis, Charles A. et al. Agroecology: The Ecology of Food Systems. Journal of Sustainable Agriculture. 22: 99-118 (2003).*

6   *Patel, Raj. Stuffed and Starved: The Hidden Battle for the World Food System. Brooklyn, NY: Melville House Publishing. April 2008.*

7   *Jefferson, Thomas. Notes on the State of Virginia.Published: 1781–1782.*

8   *Personal communication with Eric Holt-Giménez, Executive Director, Food First/Institute for Food & Development Policy. January 26, 2011.*

However, the food chain provides employment for millions of workers in other sectors, some unseen to the eye of the consumer, such as processing and distribution. A movement based on a holistic understanding of food justice needs to encompass the chain of food production that connects seeds to mouths. The food chain includes the workers that help to plant the seeds, harvest the crops, package the food, deliver the product and serve the meal to consumers. The future of good food must not ignore these workers and their livelihoods. Food justice must involve increasing their wages and improving their working conditions, so that they too can enjoy healthy and sustainable lives.

People of color are often limited to low-wage jobs in the food industry, especially recent and undocumented immigrants who can easily find seasonal work harvesting crops in the fields. At least six out of every 10 farmworkers is an undocumented immigrant.[9] Also, the food industry continues to grow even during economic recession, offering more job opportunities. The nation, as a whole, lost 1.9 percent of jobs between December 2007 and December 2008, yet the restaurant industry only contracted by 0.5 percent in the same time frame.[10]

> A movement for food justice must advocate for dignity and respect for the workers who help to produce, process, distribute and serve us our food....

Often, workers in the food chain suffer low wages and exploitative conditions. Farm labor, for example, has a higher rate of toxic chemical injuries than workers in any other sector of the U.S. economy, with an estimated 300,000 farmworkers suffering from pesticide poisoning annually.[11] Service workers in the restaurant industry, which serves food to consumers at the end of the chain, face unfair labor practices ranging from employers withholding wages to not getting paid for overtime.[12] Also, many sectors of the food chain are excluded from the protections of federal labor laws. This includes farmworkers, tipped minimum wage workers

9   Southern Poverty Law Center. *Injustice on our Plates: Immigrant Women in the U.S. Food Industry.* November 2010.

10 Restaurant Opportunities Center of New York and New York City Restaurant Industry Coalition. *The Great Service Divide: Occupational Segregation and Inequality in the New York City Restaurant Industry.* March 31, 2009.

11 *Like Machines in the Fields: Workers Without Rights in American Agriculture.* OxFam America (2004), p. 2-3.

12 Bernhardt, Annette et al. *Broken Laws, Unprotected Workers: Violations of Employment and Labor Laws in America's Cities.* September 2009. www.unprotectedworkers.org

such as those in restaurants, and the formerly incarcerated. These workers fall under the rubric of excluded workers, who lack the right to organize without retaliation, because they are excluded from labor law protection or the laws are not enforced.[13]

...This will require us to build meaningful and durable bridges between the food, labor and racial justice movements.

Food workers also suffer from lack of access to healthy food. Numerous studies document high rates of food insecurity, malnutrition and hunger among farmworkers. In California, a 2007 study found that 45 percent of surveyed agricultural workers were food insecure, and nearly half were on food stamps.[14] A similar survey in North Carolina documented that over 63 percent of migrant and seasonal farmworkers were food insecure, with almost 35 percent experiencing hunger.[15]

Description of the Food Chain Workers Alliance

The Food Chain Workers Alliance is a coalition of worker-based organizations whose members plant, harvest, process, pack, transport, prepare, serve and sell food, organizing to improve wages and working conditions for all workers along the food chain. The Alliance was founded in July 2009. By coming together in the Alliance, members have greater power to improve the wages and working and living conditions of food workers and their families.

The Alliance also challenges institutionalized racism and strives to balance the immense corporate power over our food system in order to work towards ending poverty and therefore hunger, and to truly achieve food sovereignty, sustainable food production, environmental justice, and respect for workers' and community rights. Members of the Alliance include Restaurant Opportunities Centers United, Center for New Community, the Coalition of Immokalee Workers and Brandworkers International.

---

13   *Unity for Dignity: Expanding the Right to Organize to Win Human Rights at Work. Excluded Workers Congress. December 2010.*

14   *Wirth, Cathy et al. ˙Hunger in the Fields: Food Insecurity among Farmworkers in Fresno County." California Institute for Rural Studies. November 2007.*

15   *Borre, Kristen et al. ˙Working to eat: Vulnerability, food insecurity, and obesity among migrant and seasonal farmworker families." American Journal of Industrial Medicine, 53: 443–462 (2010).*

This report is intended to support the collaborative efforts of advocates and researchers—such as those at the Food Chain Workers Alliance, the Data Center and Food First—who are working diligently to bring attention to the invisible labor that populate the food supply chain. Like these advocates, ARC is committed to identifying solutions through which food workers can make their jobs and lives sustainable for themselves and their families.

The Color of Food explores the universe of workers that populate the food chain, from food's inception as seed to when it reaches our plates at home or in a restaurant. Generally, such broad explorations of the color and gender of the food workforce have been rare. This mapping of the race, class and gender of food workers provides a baseline from which the food justice movement can dream of a new supply chain, one that sustains and nourishes its labor, as well as its consumers.

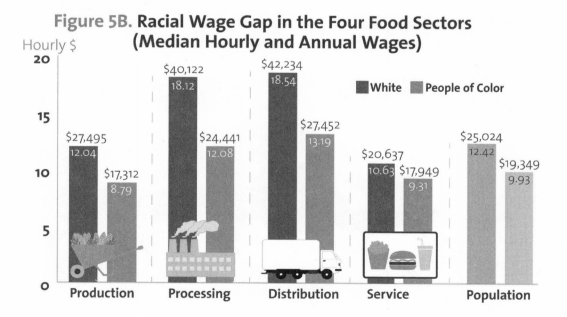

Figure 5B. Racial Wage Gap in the Four Food Sectors (Median Hourly and Annual Wages)

Graphic courtesy of the Applied Research Center, "The Color of Food," by Yvonne Yen Liu & Dominique Apollon, PhD.

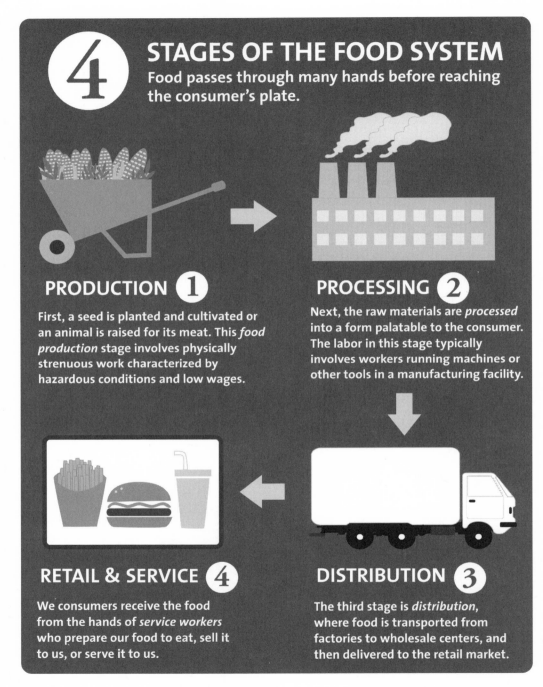

4 STAGES OF THE FOOD SYSTEM
Food passes through many hands before reaching the consumer's plate.

PRODUCTION 1

First, a seed is planted and cultivated or an animal is raised for its meat. This *food production* stage involves physically strenuous work characterized by hazardous conditions and low wages.

PROCESSING 2

Next, the raw materials are *processed* into a form palatable to the consumer. The labor in this stage typically involves workers running machines or other tools in a manufacturing facility.

RETAIL & SERVICE 4

We consumers receive the food from the hands of *service workers* who prepare our food to eat, sell it to us, or serve it to us.

DISTRIBUTION 3

The third stage is *distribution*, where food is transported from factories to wholesale centers, and then delivered to the retail market.

Download these and further graphics in the extended report at: www.arc.org/content/view/2229/136/

Figure 7A. Distribution of Managers and Annual Median Wage

■ White ■ People of Color

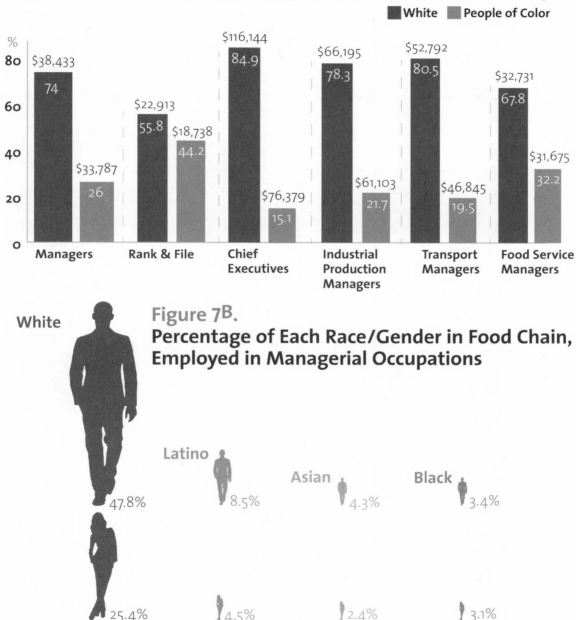

Figure 7B.
Percentage of Each Race/Gender in Food Chain, Employed in Managerial Occupations

White 47.8%

Latino 8.5%

Asian 4.3%

Black 3.4%

25.4% 4.5% 2.4% 3.1%

All graphics courtesy of the Applied Research Center, "The Color of Food," by Yvonne Yen Liu & Dominique Apollon, PhD.

31

Moving Forward

For many, the impulse to eat "good food"—be it artisan-crafted bread, goat cheese purchased directly from the maker, or eggs from a hen in a family's backyard—is a reaction against the industrialization and corporate control of the food system. Increasing numbers of consumers are demanding locally grown food, without pesticides or hormones, and either raising their own food or cultivating relationships with the producers of their edibles.

A movement for food justice must advocate for the dignity of and respect for the workers who help to produce, process, distribute and serve us our food. This will require us to build meaningful and durable bridges between the food, labor and racial justice movements.

Figure 6. Race and Gender in the Food Chain

Race & Gender	Ratio of Median Annual Wages
White Men $1.00	
Asian Men $0.83	
Black Men $0.71	
Asian Women $0.68	
Latino Men $0.66	
White Women $0.63	
Black Women $0.53	
Latina Women $0.50	

This report establishes that racial disparity in wages and representation can be found in most occupations along the food chain. This is baseline data, which should be tracked both backwards and forwards, seeing if there are trends in the composition of the food workforce over time. This will be particularly important when key legislation is implemented that impacts the flow of labor into and out of the food industry.

Graphic courtesy of the Applied Research Center, "The Color of Food," by Yvonne Yen Liu & Dominique Apollon, PhD.

A pattern of stringent anti-immigration laws—such as the one recently enacted in Arizona—will hinder recent and undocumented immigrants as well as people of color perceived to be undocumented immigrants from seeking work in many parts of the country, unless more can be done to articulate and advocate for a functioning, sane and humane immigration system that respects the human dignity of workers, including those whose labor is so critical to the food we consume on a daily basis.

More funding is needed for research to establish working conditions and career mobility in the food chain. Government data cannot help to identify the career pathway of food workers. However, interviews with workers can be carried out in the four sectors to understand job stability in a food-related occupation and whether advancement in the food sector is possible. Employers also need to be surveyed to see what factors play into whether they hire or promote a worker.

Food workers need more opportunities to take leadership in defining what is good for them and their families. Sustainability can take the form of higher wages, health and retirement benefits, safe and healthy working conditions, and opportunities for advancement. This is action research that needs to be done in every sector of the food industry to ensure that the entire system sustains its producers, as well as its consumers.

The Applied Research Center (ARC) is a racial justice think tank and home for media and activism. ARC is built on rigorous research and creative use of new technology. Their goal is to popularize the need for racial justice and prepare people to fight for it. By telling the stories of everyday people, ARC is a voice for unity and fairness in the structures that affect our lives. Find them at **www.arc.org**

Digging Deeper for Food Justice:

Engaging Latino Immigrants in Social Movements for Sustainable Food

Teresa M. Mares, Ph.D., founding Food Justice Project Co-Chair

This piece is based upon a section of the author's 2010 dissertation, "We Are Made of Our Food: Latino/a Immigration & the Practices & Politics of Eating"

Introduction

In November of 2009, I attended a talk in Seattle by Eric Holt-Giménez, Executive Director of Food First. It was November 30th, ten years to the day of the World Trade Organization protests that shut down the city in 1999, and he was speaking at the invitation of the Community Alliance for Global Justice (CAGJ). As an active member of CAGJ, I was thrilled to see the huge crowd that had turned out for the event. A decade after the "Battle of Seattle," Holt-Giménez spoke to a captivated audience about the global food crisis, the devastating impacts of free trade agreements like NAFTA for farmers in the Global South, and the inspiring ways that grassroots groups around the world were resisting the industrialization and centralization of food through organizing for food sovereignty.

Having finished a series of interviews for my dissertation research with Latino/a day-laborers earlier that week, one vignette that he shared was more relevant to me than anything else that night. He stated:

> You know, there's a sick joke amongst older farmers here because the average age of a farmer in the United States is approaching sixty right now…and the joke is, in ten years the average age of the American farmer is going to be dead. Nonetheless, this country is full of farmers! They are standing on the street corners looking for work. They come from Mexico, Honduras, Nicaragua, Guatemala, Colombia, Panama. They've been displaced! They mow our lawns, they pump our gas, they cook our food in the fancy restaurants, those are farmers. We're surrounded by farmers. They're out of work.

In these brief lines, Holt-Giménez synthesized a complex contradiction that persists in our agricultural and service sectors—connecting the increasing numbers of people moving to the U.S. in search of work with the displacement of farmers from their homes and fields in Latin America.

Research Goals

Between 2005 and 2009 I conducted fieldwork in the Seattle area on issues of urban agriculture, hunger, and food insecurity among Latino/a immigrants. In addition to archival research, this included conducting participant observation and two sets of semi-structured interviews. In the first set, I spoke with representatives from thirteen agencies around the Seattle area, including direct service organizations, organizations working in urban agriculture, and institutions doing food systems work from a standpoint of political advocacy. In the second set, I interviewed 46 first-generation immigrants who have moved to the U.S. from various regions of Latin America, with an equal number of men and women. I asked these participants about their experiences growing food, both in their home countries and in the US, their perspectives on health and eating, and their experiences with different agencies in the Seattle food system. Here, I use pseudonyms for everyone I interviewed.

"This country is full of farmers! We're surrounded by farmers. They are standing on the street corners looking for work."

Over the course of my fieldwork, I was struck by how rapidly the Seattle food system was changing. Surrounded by some of the richest farmland in the nation and characterized by exceptionally favorable climatic conditions, Seattle has become a hotbed for food systems work and food movements. While I was excited by these changes that were taking place and took great delight in choosing from the heirloom varieties of tomatoes and apples that appeared each weekend at my neighborhood farmers market, I couldn't shake my observations that access to these alternative food spaces was clearly limited for the working class and communities of color. The narratives that Latino/a participants shared with me about their eating and growing practices only reinforced these observations.

Despite the exciting ways that the local food system is being transformed for some Seattle residents, there is much work to be done to increase Latino/a involvement. Out of the 46 participants from Latin America, only four were growing food in the city, with an additional three growing herbs. Only eight mentioned shopping at the farmer's markets, even while many shared memories of doing their daily shopping at open-air markets close to their Latin American homes. None of the Latino/a participants mentioned CSA programs.

In the midst of dislocation, maintaining and re-creating cultural practices related to food are powerful means to assert one's cultural identity. Food is central to the longing for home.

However, my research also revealed that the majority of interviewees had grown food in their home countries and the memories of the gardens and farms they cultivated often brought smiles to their faces and prompted stories of time spent with their families and the sharing of recipes. Of the 46, 37 had grown food before moving to the U.S., including those who had lived in rural and urban areas, from northern Mexico to the highlands of Peru.

The low participation in urban agriculture in the U.S., despite a high level of agri-food knowledge and experience in their home countries, signals multiple barriers preventing people from being engaged in community food projects and the social movements that push them forward. In the remainder of this short article, I would like to focus on the barriers present in urban agricultural practices and what they mean for food movements in the Seattle area.

First, there is little doubt that the groups working in the local food system are full of staff members who are both committed to building more just food systems and see the potential in working more with Latino immigrants who have deep knowledge about growing food. More often than not, their ability to carry out these commitments is constrained by the histories and structures that govern the institutions for whom they work. Ruth, who works with an organization dedicated to organic gardening education, had this to say:

> *It seems kind of obvious, and I don't want to jinx us, but there is the challenge of being a historically white organization. I think that's our challenge in general. It's a historically white organization. But our world is changing at a very rapid pace, and a lot of things that are historically white are changing…*

36

Well, like, any white, historically white place, it's a monoculture! And we teach about that, but we're not even following our own curriculum to diversity! Because that's what we teach, that any biological system is a stronger one if it's more diverse, so honestly, I think the organization will fail if it's not able to diversify! … [B]ecause, in practical terms what it might mean is a lot of new growing techniques, new crops, new solutions to problems, new approaches to food production in an increasingly urbanized area. I mean, we are all kind of inventing a whole new thing together, really.

Ruth understands that more inclusive involvement in gardening projects would mean an infusion of new knowledge and new solutions, potentially transforming the local food system into something more relevant and meaningful for immigrant families and communities.

This possibility was echoed by Latino/a participants who expressed their frustration over having to buy all of their food in the United States, rather than growing and harvesting it on their own. I asked Arturo, who had lived in several different states over a span of fifteen years, if he felt that he was able to afford less fresh food in Seattle than he had in Mexico, to which he responded,

What happens, for example, in Mexico, in the fields, for example, vegetables are in the fields, or lettuces, tomatoes, all of that. Limes, you cut them from the trees at your house. But here, you have to buy everything. In the city you have to buy everything. It could be cheap, but it's not cheap, because you have to buy everything!

Having been born and raised in the federal district of Mexico, Arturo's roots extended to the fields of Michoacan. He was one of the few men that tended a garden in Seattle, a small space near his home where he grows tomatoes, garlic, onions, and flowers. The food that he grew here allowed him some autonomy over his diet, but did not provide a sizeable proportion of his diet or a way to connect with the broader food movements.

Vanesa, the mother of five children who had lived in the U.S. for sixteen years, told me about the deep knowledge that she had gained through growing food while living in Mexico. Her grandfather had owned 55 hectares of land, but had to sell it when he was no longer able to make a living as a farmer. Living in a small

Read more about women's roles in the food system, in Erica Bacon's "Feminine Fortitude in the World Food System: Women's Contribution to Food Sovereignty" on p. 118.

37

apartment with family, she has been able to take advantage of the small amount of land she has near her apartment and apply (with varying success) the lessons she had learned on her grandfather's land. She related, "I tried last year to garden. I planted some squash, some zucchinis, the big green ones. And I took such good care of them, but nothing! I had to cut them! But it could be so beautiful!"

While both Vanesa and Arturo had experimented with growing at a small scale, neither of them had participated in, or were even aware of, the possibility of joining the community gardens in their area, or the opportunities to learn more about the unique climate and growing season of the Pacific Northwest.

Conclusion

In the midst of dislocation, maintaining and re-creating cultural and material practices related to food are powerful means to assert one's cultural identity and sustain membership with communities that are not physically present. Likewise, food is central to the longing for home and the painful struggles to accommodate new ways of being in the world. However, as Vanesa and Arturo's lives reveal, the disruptive process of migration necessarily brings about radical changes in diet, community membership, and social standing. As agri-food scholars have repeatedly shown, addressing fundamental inequalities that are bound to the commodification of food is not necessarily a strongpoint of the movements for local food and community food security (Allen 2008, Allen and Wilson 2008).

To learn more about the meaning of food sovereignty, see "The Seven Principles of Food Sovereignty" on p. 18.

The need for a deeper, transnational analysis of the food system and more radical visions of transformation is met in part by the movements for *food justice* and *food sovereignty*. The concept of food sovereignty pays particular attention to the struggles and rights of third world peasant farmers (especially women), the impacts of neoliberal trade and agricultural policies, and the importance of working in solidarity across international borders.

Food sovereignty's emphasis on rights and issues of control shifts the focus beyond the equitable provisioning of food to address more fundamental inequalities related to land distribution, resource management, and exploitation. Although the food sovereignty movement has largely developed through the mobilization

of rural peasant farmers, agri-food scholars and activists see great potential in furthering the movement in urban contexts (Schiavoni 2009). What then, might a framework of food sovereignty add to the food movements in Seattle?

First, food sovereignty transcends the boundaries of the local to demand consideration of the impacts of industrialization and centralization on local food economies everywhere, forging an interdependent connection between local food systems in Seattle to local food systems around the world. It draws attention to the political and economic forces that displace small farmers in Latin America and other regions of the Global South. In this way, it acknowledges the denigration of displaced farmers who have no choice but to migrate by recognizing the ways that their autonomy and livelihoods have been compromised against their will.

By integrating a food sovereignty framework into the growing food movements in Seattle, the struggles of displaced Latino/a famers could potentially be better understood and their food and farming experiences better acknowledged. As Ruth emphasized, diverse growing practices and sets of knowledge could only improve the likelihood of transforming the local food system into one that is more inclusive, resilient, and indeed, more sovereign.

Focusing on food sovereignty would allow Seattle's food movements to go beyond the framework of "cultural appropriateness," to really consider the cultural importance of food in sustaining social relationships and how food can be implicitly used to erode social relationships, cultural meaning, connections to place, and the exercising of rights. Finally, it would allow food activists to more accurately locate the sources of the injustices they rally against and more specifically challenge the limitations of a market-dominated system of food production and consumption.

Teresa Mares was the founding Food Justice Project Co-Chair. She lives in Burlington, Vermont where she is enjoying her new job as an assistant professor in anthropology at the University of Vermont.

Traditional Foods of Puget Sound Project

Elise Krohn, herbalist & wild food educator

with material from "Feeding the People, Feeding the Spirit" by Elise Krohn & Valerie Segrest

In the Squaxin Island Tribe of the Medicine Creek Nation it was common for our people to live beyond 100 years old. Tribal elders attribute this longevity to knowledge about traditional foods and medicines that was passed down from generation to generation. Their powerful traditional science included understanding techniques for gathering, knowing when was the most potent time to harvest, how food was processed for everyday use and how plants were used for ceremonial purposes. This knowledge was highly regarded as a sacred gift that contributed to living a long and fulfilling life.

—Charlene Krise, Squaxin Island Tribe

Introduction

Almost every tribal community in Western Washington has stories of relatives who lived to be over 100 years old. Often they are remembered for gathering and growing their own food. This practice has been passed down for countless generations. It has been a way of life that both sustains people and creates a rich culture. As archeological research has confirmed, Northwest Coastal Indian ancestors ate a great variety of foods before European contact (Puget Sound Traditional Foods and Diabetes Project, n.d.). The land was rich with fish, shellfish, wild game, berries, fruits, wild greens, nuts and roots. As the seasons changed, people traveled to places where special foods were abundant. Those foods were often processed and preserved for later use. Food was and continues to be a living part of the culture—a direct link with the land. Cultural protocols have been followed for fishing, hunting, gathering, preparing and eating. Elders say these protocols protect natural resources and insure continued abundance.

Historically, gathering food and sharing it with family and community was woven into everyday life. Food brought people together over a common purpose. Stories and laughter were shared while hands processed fish, berries, and nuts. As Dr.

Rudy Ryser from the Cowlitz Indian Tribe said, "The kitchen table was a place where cultural knowledge was passed from one generation to the next."

In just a few generations, Northwest Coastal Indian peoples' ability to eat their traditional foods has declined. Important foods, including camas, soapberry, gooseberry and eulachon that were commonly eaten are now diffi-cult or nearly impossible to find. Elders from many communities are saddened that they can no longer harvest and prepare the foods they grew up eating. The implications of this are vast. As the availability of these foods has declined, the stories and language connected to them fall silent. Invaluable aspects of the culture are lost.

Northwest Coastal Indian peoples' health has also suffered from a loss of traditional foods. Type 2 diabetes was virtually non-existent among Northwest Coastal Indian people about 125 years ago. Dur-ing colonization, native foods, which are rich in complex nutrients, were replaced with commodity foods that are high in carbohydrates, sugar, dairy and poor quality fats. Today, Native American communities are at greater risk for diabetes than other groups; having American Indian or Alaskan Native heritage is one of the top risk factors. Currently, the prevalence of dia-betes among Native Americans is several times higher than that of the general population.

Many people believe that traditional foods can help prevent the chronic diseas-es that are so prevalent among Indian people today. It is generally agreed upon by researchers that when native people eat the foods that their ancestors relied on for countless generations, they are less likely to suffer from chronic diseases including diabetes, heart disease and cancer. Some of the solutions to prevent-ing modern chronic diseases are clear: eat healthier foods and have a more traditional lifestyle that includes exercise.

When native people eat the foods that their ancestors relied on for countless generations, they are less likely to suffer from chronic diseases including diabetes, heart disease and cancer.

The Traditional Foods of Puget Sound Project

In 2008–2010 the Northwest Indian College's Cooperative Extension Department conducted a community-based participatory research project called the Traditional Foods of Puget Sound Project. The research team included traditional plants and foods specialists Elise Krohn and Valerie Segrest. They worked with scores of tribal service providers and cooks to address this question: *How do we utilize research about traditional foods of Puget Sound Indians to create a healthier diet and lifestyle for Indian people today?* Throughout the project, barriers and solutions were documented that will ultimately help improve the health of Northwest Coastal Indian people by increasing their access to traditional foods and healthy local foods.

Traditional Food Principles

Elise Krohn & Valerie Segrest

When we talked with elders and traditional foods specialists about what a modern traditional foods diet might look like, a revitalized way of thinking about food emerged. As elders discussed their cultural beliefs around food, we noticed that many Indian people hold common values that are as applicable today as they were generations ago. We call these Traditional Foods Principles. They address the physical and spiritual health of individuals and communities in conjunction with the well-being of the land.

Food is at the Center of Culture

People traditionally harvested, processed, prepared and shared meals together. This unity is an integral part of cultural identity. During colonization, this important part of culture changed dramatically as many traditional foods were no longer available and cultural traditions around food were suppressed. This changed the family dynamics around how people spend time together. People understood that food is precious, is a gift from nature, and is necessary for our existence. Eating foods in this way helps feed the desire for wholeness within us, and it can be amplified when the entire family participates in a meal together. Individuals can become nourished and enriched, as they partake in a fundamental aspect of survival with the ones they love, and the family becomes strengthened. For example, our ancestors used the whole animal, and the sharing of that animal by a group of people strengthened the connections that held them together. Eating collectively can also be a time when culture is transmitted from one generation to the next through conversation and leading by example.

Honor the Food Web/Chain

Living in harmony with nature is a native teaching. As we know, everything is connected. It must be remembered that the ramifications of polluting our soil and our water can be seen in the health of plants, animals and ultimately us. We have a responsibility to maintain the health of our food system as our ancestors did, so that we pass down a world that will support the generations to come.

Eat with the Seasons

A traditional food diet is diverse and is based on the seasons. The power of being in the moment and harvesting what is available ensures that a variety of foods will be on the menu. Seasonal foods prepared people for seasonal changes as well. For example, eating nettles in spring helps your body to cleanse and detoxify after eating winter foods.

Eat a Variety of Foods

Most Americans currently eat less than 12 foods on a regular basis. Our ancestors ate more complex foods and received a greater variety of vitamins and minerals in their diet. Eating many types of foods also helped preserve the diversity of the environment, which helped uphold the entire ecosystem by avoiding over harvesting of any one resource. We know that healthy ecosystems are diverse ones. Now that people are eating very few foods due to mass monocrops like corn, wheat and soy, we are losing environmental diversity.

Traditional Foods are Whole Foods

Traditional foods are "real foods" that have grown in nature. They are not industrialized foods that have been refined or contain additives, dyes or chemicals. A whole food is alive, and consists of one ingredient, itself. Living things eventually decompose, so if your food does not rot, it is not good for you (e.g., Twinkies and McNuggets). If you don't understand the ingredients in a food, you probably should not eat it. You should not need a science degree to understand food labels. If you cannot picture an ingredient growing in nature, it most likely is not food at all. Think of going to the grocery store with your ancestors a few generations back. What would they recognize as food?

Eat Local Foods

Plants breathe, respire and require water. After they are cut off from their food source, they begin to die, which means they are losing nutrients and flavor. Therefore, eating fresh food is really important. Think of how you feel after traveling—exhausted, dehydrated, drained, low energy. Food gets tired from travel as well. The best foods for our health are fresh foods. Eating local is also good for the environment because it reduces the amount of fossil fuels used to transport food to us, and helps support our local economy.

Wild and Organic Foods are Better for Health

Wild foods are denser in nutrients and lower in calories. Processed and refined foods (e.g. high fructose corn syrup) tend to provide empty calories and may only offer a part of a food. This contributes to weight gain as our body, in its natural wisdom, craves all the missing parts of processed and refined foods. Organic foods also guarantee that we are getting all the nutrients essential for our bodies. Intensive agricultural practices deplete mineral content in the soil and therefore in the plants that grow from the soil. When we eat wild and organic foods, we are supporting a healthier body and environment.

Cook and Eat with Good Intention

Eating is a reminder that we are human. Cooking is a time to honor the foods we eat. It is a time to pay respect to the life that has been given to nourish our bodies. We are connected to the food culture around us. The food we consume ties us into our place and our purpose in that place. Good intention becomes a part of what we prepare, serve and consume. It is important to thank the plants and animals that gave their lives to sustain yours. The way we eat is just as important as what we eat. We are frequently eating while on the go and hurrying on to the next task. This takes the pleasure out of eating and it doesn't allow our bodies sufficient time to relax enough to savor and digest, leaving us hungry for more. Reflect on what you consume, as well as how you consume your meals.

Eating traditionally means eating different local foods at different times of year, as they ripen with the seasons. A spring basket will hold a variety of foods distinct from those in an autumn basket.

drawing by Roger Fernandes

45

Ways to increase access to traditional foods:

While many tribal people speak about great loss around traditional foods, there is also great hope in what remains intact. Many families and communities are revitalizing their traditional food systems in order to improve the health and well-being of their people.

Many families and communities are revitalizing their traditional food systems in order to improve the health and well-being of their people.

Community food security emerged as a topic throughout the research project. Northwest Coastal Indian people historically ate many types of seasonal foods from a variety of ecosystems. Because of this, you could say that their ability to access good food was fairly stable. If there was a bad salmon run, people could rely on other types of seafood. If it was a bad berry year for one kind of berry, people might be able to substitute another of the many types of wild berries and fruits. The greater the diversity of foods people ate, the better their health was, and the more secure their food supply.

The terms *food sustainability* and *food sovereignty* are used to describe whether a community has access to high quality local food. *Sustainability* is the capacity to endure over time. In nature, this means that biological systems need to remain diverse and productive. People live sustainably when they take care of the natural resources that support them. *Sovereignty* is the ability to have supreme independent authority over a territory. Therefore, communities that have *food sustainability and food sovereignty:*

- Have access to healthy food
- Have foods that are culturally appropriate
- Grow, gather, hunt or fish in a way that is maintainable over the long-term
- Distribute foods in ways so that people get what they need to stay healthy
- Adequately compensate the people who provide the food

According to many of the research participants, tribal communities often rely on government commodities and state and federal food programs. The food provided is often high in sugar, carbohydrates and poor quality fats, increasing the risk of developing diabetes and other chronic diseases. Fresh produce and good quality proteins and fats that were the foundation to a healthy traditional diet are not

46

as available in these food programs. Additionally, state and federal food programs often mandate what types of foods must be served, even if they are not culturally appropriate. This is where the importance of food sovereignty is evident. When tribal communities are able to produce more of their own healthy food, they will be less restricted by food regulations. There are many reasons that tribal communities may want to become more stable in their ability to provide their own food. According to the Food Sovereignty Assessment Tool designed by the First Nations Development Institute (2004):

> *Assuming power to localize your food supply affords opportunities to regain control of the most significant assets possessed by Native communities. Conscious management of food supplies affords opportunities for tribal use of land, deliberate control of health, sustainability of the environment, and maintenance or revitalization of cultural integrity.*

photo by Elise Krohn

Northwest Indian College Cooperative Extension, Traditional Plants and Foods Program seaweed class, hosted by the Lower Elwha Klallam Tribe, near Port Angeles, WA.

Food Restoration Programs

In the Traditional Foods of Puget Sound Project, research participants were asked how they might increase access to traditional foods. People shared many exciting ideas and current projects. Some of these included:

- **Community food gardens** where people can learn to plant, grow, harvest & cook with both native and non-native fruits and vegetables
- **Pea Patch Gardens or small family gardens**
- **Native food restoration projects** that will help recover plants, fish, shellfish and other native food populations
- **Community food banks** where hunters, fisherman and gatherers can donate extra food to elders and other community members
- **Partnerships with the U.S. Forest Service, Department of Natural Resources and private land owners** that allow tribal people access to traditional harvesting areas
- **Partnerships with local farmers** who are willing to supply produce to tribal communities

One woman who fishes for a living reminded people of how important it is to get to know people who gather, hunt or fish in their communities. Often they are willing to donate food for tribal events or may also be willing to trade. People spoke of how we all have different gifts and it is good to rely on each other. This helps build a strong community, and when we recognize our dependence on the environment and on other people, we can take up our responsibilities to maintain those relationships and pass them on to the next generation.

photo by Elise Krohn

Harvesting camas for a traditional dinner.

photo by Elise Krohn

Northwest Indian College Cooperative Extension Tribal Cooks Camp.
Cooking is a time to celebrate the joy of sharing, and good feelings are
essential ingredients in preparing traditional foods.

*For more photos of
the people and the
foods at the center
of the Salish Sea's
cultural renaissance
around traditional
diets and traditions,
see the color photo
section of this book.*

*Elise Krohn lives in Olympia, WA and works for the Northwest Indian College
Cooperative Extension, teaching about the many wondrous uses for wild foods and
medicines. Elise is the author of "Wild Rose and Western Red Cedar: the Gifts of the
Northwest Plants." Her independent wild foods blog can be found at:*
www.wildfoodsandmedicines.com

*Valerie Segrest is a Native nutrition educator who specializes in local and traditional
foods of the Puget Sound region. Valerie teaches classes on traditional foods and
medicines for the Northwest Indian College's Cooperative Extension Department,
and coordinates the Muckleshoot Food Sovereignty Project. Her blog can be found at:*
www.feedingthespirit.org

*In 2010 Elise and Valerie co-authored the book "Feeding the People, Feeding the
Spirit: Revitalizing Northwest Coastal Indian Food Culture."*

Domestic Fair Trade Association Makes Strides
to Revive Social Justice in Sustainable & Organic Agriculture

Erin Thompson, Domestic Fair Trade Association, and Director of Food Sovereignty Programs, Community to Community Development in Bellingham, WA

Introduction

In recent years, the Fair Trade movement has united farmers, workers, traders and consumers with a message of fairness, equity and environmental stewardship in trade with producers in marginalized countries. Representing a convergence of cooperative, solidarity, and social justice movements, Fair Trade emphasizes ownership, empowerment and development for small-scale farmers, artisans and workers in the global South.

Increasingly, the challenges faced by rural communities are very similar around the world. The movement for Domestic Fair Trade is gaining momentum and member organizations of the Domestic Fair Trade Association (DFTA) have come together to advocate for and practice a fair, equitable, and sustainable agricultural system that supports family-scale farms, farmer-led initiatives such as farmer co-ops, just conditions for workers, and organic and other environmental standards for agriculture.

At the DFTA, we seek to bring these efforts together with mission-based traders, retailers and consumers to contribute to the movement for more equitable, diverse and sustainable agriculture in North America and around the world. By creating businesses committed to principles of fairness and equity and leading by example, we hope to create positive change in the mainstream marketplace by influencing the conduct of conventional corporations.

The mission of the DFTA is to educate the public, to promote Domestic Fair Trade Principles (see opposite), to endorse Domestic Fair Trade and social justice claims and labels, and to defend endorsed labels in the marketplace. The DFTA is not a certifier and does not aspire to own a particular label. Instead, the DFTA will provide an umbrella organization under which regional fair trade labels can flourish by vetting independent labels according to the 16 articulated principles adopted by the full membership.

Vision of the DFTA:

We envision an agricultural and economic system that is a healthy community where all look after and support each other, everyone feels safe, and all contribute to and benefit from a clean and harmonious environment. Family-scale and community-scale farms and businesses thrive. All people recognize the realities, challenges and effects of production, distribution and labor and choose to participate in fair trade.

Our vision includes a world where:

- Contributions of all workers and farmers are valued
- Human rights and human dignity are affirmed and promoted
- Fair Trade is synonymous with fair wages, fair prices, and fair practices
- Risks and rewards are equitable and shared, and this information is open and available to all stakeholders
- Information is readily available on the origin, processing, and distribution of every product
- All practices are environmentally, economically, and socially just, sustainable, and humane
- Direct trade and long-term relationships dominate the economy
- Strong local communities are the foundation of society
- Power is shared; development is community-driven and cooperative
- Cultural and indigenous rights and diversity are recognized, honored, and protected.

Membership

A core value of the DFTA is stakeholder representation and as such is open to mission-based organizations in five stakeholder categories:

Farmers and Farmer Cooperatives. Family and small-scale farmers and democratic farmers' cooperatives that serve and represent them.

Farm Workers' Organizations. Organizations representing agricultural workers, and particularly those with an agrarian vision that includes farm labor and small producers.

Food Processing and Marketing Enterprises. Food processors and marketers with a mission of promoting fair trade, sustainable agriculture, and social justice.

Food Retailers and Consumer Co-ops. Retailers with a mission of supporting family farming and sustainable agriculture, connecting small producers with consumers, and making such activities a significant part of their business.

Civil Society Organizations and NGOs. Community-based organizations that advocate for Fair Trade, sustainable agriculture, social justice, and conscientious consumption in the food system.

In the process of applying for membership to the DFTA, all potential members are asked to assess their organizational performance on each of the 16 principles. Organizations are also asked to identify goals for improvement in particular areas. Local members include Farm Worker Organization stakeholder Community to Community Development in Bellingham, WA and a Retail stakeholder, the Olympia Food Co-op in Olympia, WA.

Principles

The 16 principles of the DFTA as currently adopted attempt to translate the traditional principles of international fair trade, as expressed by organizations such as the World Fair Trade Organization (WFTO) and the Fair Trade Federation (FTF), into the domestic, regional and local economic spheres. It is our hope that by maintaining a consistent approach that shares basic values with international fair trade, we may help create a more holistic model, which can in turn be applied wherever trade takes place. These principles represent the values which underlie and guide our work together as organizations and individuals united for the promotion of "Health, Justice and Sustainability."

Family Scale Farming.

Fair Trade focuses on reinforcing the position of small and family-scale producers that have been or are being marginalized by the mainstream marketplace, as a means of preserving the culture of farming and rural communities, promoting economic democracy, environmental and humane stewardship and biodiversity, and ensuring a healthier and more sustainable planet.

Capacity Building for Producers and Workers.

Fair Trade is a means of developing producers' and workers' independence, strengthening their ability to engage directly with the marketplace, and gaining more control over their futures. The resources from trading relationships are directed toward this purpose in a participatory manner by those who will benefit from them.

"Free trade" does not mean "fair trade"! To learn about how trade policy impacts farmers around the world, see "Farmers at the Table: Connecting Food and Trade Justice" on p. 102

Democratic & Participatory Ownership & Control.

Fair Trade emphasizes co-operative organization as a means of empowering producers, workers, and consumers to gain more control over their economic and social lives. In situations where such organization is absent, mechanisms will be created to ensure the democratic participation of producers and workers, and the equitable distribution of the fruits of trade.

Rights of Labor.

Fair Trade means a safe and healthy working environment for producers and workers and conforms to all International Labour Organization conventions and the Universal Declaration of Human Rights. The participation of children (if any) does not adversely affect their well-being, security, educational requirements and need for play, and conforms to the United Nations Convention on the Rights of the Child as well as pertinent local and regional laws. Fair Trade ensures that there are mechanisms in place through which hired labor has an independent voice and is included in the benefits of trade through mechanisms such as living wages, profit sharing, and cooperative workplace structures. Apprenticeships are promoted to develop the skills of the next generation of farmers, artisans, and workers.

Equality & Opportunity.

Fair Trade emphasizes the empowerment of women, minorities, indigenous peoples and other marginalized members of society to represent their own interests, to participate directly in trade, and to share in its economic benefits.

Direct Trade.

Where possible, Fair Trade attempts to reduce the intermediaries between the primary producer and the consumer. This delivers more of the benefits of such trade to the producer and connects consumers more directly with the source of their food and other products, and with the people who produced them.

Fair & Stable Pricing.

A fair price is one which has been agreed upon through dialogue and participation. It covers not only the costs of production but enables production which is socially just and environmentally sound. It provides fair pay to the producers, fair wages to workers, and takes into account the principle of equal pay for equal work by women and men. Fair Traders ensure prompt payment and stable pricing which enables producers to plan for the future.

Shared Risk & Affordable Credit.

Farmers often bear the greatest risks of agriculture and an unstable marketplace. Fair Traders work to share these risks among producers, processors, marketers and consumers through more equitable trade partnerships, fair and prompt payment, transparent relationships and affordable credit. In situations where access to credit is difficult, or the terms of credit are not beneficial to producers, Fair Traders provide or facilitate access to such credit, or assist producers in creating their own mechanisms for providing credit.

Long-Term Trade Relationships.

Fair Trade fosters long-term trade partnerships at all levels within the production, processing and marketing chain that provides producers with stability and opportunities to develop marketing, production and quality skills, as well as access to new markets for their products.

Sustainable Agriculture.

Fair Trade emphasizes a holistic approach to agriculture, as defined by food sovereignty organization Via Campesina to include fishing, hunting and gathering and other means of sourcing food. Fair Trade supports sustainable agriculture practices such as organic, biodynamic, non-toxic bio-intensive integrated pest management, farm diversification, and small-scale farming which protects the environment, sustains farming communities, and provides consumers with quality, healthful food. Fair Trade emphasizes the biodiversity of traditional agriculture, supports the rights of farmers to their own seed, and preserves cultural diversity. Fair Trade also emphasizes sustainable business practices through the entire supply chain, which can include green office operations, use of alternative energies, or other sustainable practices.

Appropriate Technology.
Fair Trade supports the use of traditional technologies, which are openly and freely shared in the public domain, and excludes plants, animals, and biological processes which have been genetically engineered or modified. Further, Fair Trade discourages the use of machinery that threatens the health, safety, and employment opportunities for farmworkers and farm families.

Indigenous Peoples' Rights.
Fair Trade supports indigenous peoples' rights to access land for cultivation, fishing, hunting and gathering in customary and traditional ways, to freely exchange seeds and to retain rights to their germplasm. We fully support the right of indigenous and all peoples to food sovereignty.

Transparency & Accountability.
The Fair Trade system depends on transparency of costs, pricing and structures at all levels of the trading system. Fair Traders are accountable to each other and the wider community by openly sharing such information.

Education & Advocacy.
Fair Trade emphasizes education at all levels of the agricultural chain, engaging farmers, workers, traders and consumers in advocating for a more equitable, democratic and sustainable economy. Fair Traders in particular educate consumers about the inequities of the trading system and the need for alternatives, while sharing information with producers about the marketplace. Education strengthens the Fair Trade movement and empowers its stakeholders in creating a better world for everyone.

Responsible Certification and Marketing.
Domestic Fair Trade (DFT) should represent substantive and qualitative differences from the conventional food and agriculture system. DFT programs should be inclusive of and accountable to all stakeholders, focusing on benefiting those most

marginalized in our current food and agriculture system (such as workers and small-scale producers). Certification programs should follow good practices of third-party systems and/or participatory guarantees including complaints processes, transparency about the decision-making process, and adequate accreditation and oversight.

All market claims and labels of international or domestic fair trade, social justice, or related claims, whether part of a certification process or not, should be accurate, clear, and verifiable.

Animal Welfare.
Fair Trade ensures every animal raised for or used in production of meat, dairy, egg, honey, and other products has access to clean water, fresh air, appropriate feed, an appropriate physical environment and adequate health care. Animals on Fair Trade farms are provided with the environment, housing and diet they need to engage in natural behaviors, thereby promoting physiological and psychological health and well-being.

Evaluations

In recent years, there has been a proliferation of social justice and fair trade market claims leading to consumer confusion. Consumers are flooded with claims, many of which are not applied consistently, lack relevant meaning, or do not tell the whole story of the product or program. At the same time, many organizations and companies are making tremendous progress in setting standards for fair trade or implementing fair business practices. There is a danger that these legitimate programs and practices will become indistinguishable from false or misleading claims without a more objective consumer education and outreach campaign.

To achieve the goal of being a resource for both the public and the broader movement for assessing public market-place claims of social justice or fairness, DFTA is engaged in a process of developing criteria for domestic fair trade standards. The criteria are based on the Principles of Domestic Fair Trade and will be used to assess the validity of domestic fair trade claims and determine whether a claim is one DFTA will endorse and promote. DFTA will both identify false and misleading claims and promote programs and products that meet the high standards of the DFTA criteria process.

By providing this type of analysis, DFTA can educate consumers on the need to work towards a fair and just food and agriculture system and provide a guide to consumers wishing to support legitimate programs and products. Companies with legitimate market claims will also benefit from direct promotion by DFTA and from weakening unfair advantages of companies that make misleading or false claims. Because the ultimate goal of the DFTA criteria and endorsement process is to create lasting change in the marketplace, the criteria will also be available as a resource to companies or organizations as a framework for developing domestic fair trade programs or standards.

North America Fair Trade Stakeholder Council Forms to Clarify the Direction of Fair Trade

With Fair Trade experiencing monumental change in the past few months, some committed stakeholders in North America started a dialogue initiative in December of 2011 to clarify the direction for the Fair Trade movement in North America with

Photo by Lisa Sass Zaragoza

REPRESENTATIVES OF FARMWORKERS' ORGANIZATIONS AT THE DFTA ANNUAL MEETING IN SANTA CRUZ IN DECEMBER 2010. ERIN THOMPSON *(2nd from left) is Director of Food Sovereignty Programs at Community to Community Development.* ROSALINDA GUILLEN *(center) founded Community to Community Development, based in Bellingham, WA, and was the lead organizer on the Chateau Ste. Michelle United Farm Worker campaign (see next page).*

the goal of upholding its benefits for marginalized producers around the world. The initiative, called the North America Fair Trade Stakeholder Council, will begin with around 50 nonprofits, advocacy organizations, committed companies, producer/farmer/worker groups, academics and others, who will hold conference calls and email discussions over several months before attending an in-person summit April 30—May 2, 2012 in Minneapolis, MN. Fair Trade Resource Network (FTRN), Fair World Project (FWP), and Domestic Fair Trade Association (DFTA) comprise the Organizing Committee leading the initiative.

At present, the Council seeks to advance these 4 goals:

- **Define fair trade and the movement, what they are and what they are not**
- **Organize the North American fair trade movement under a coordinated infrastructure with a common vision**
- **Reach an agreement on a plan for cooperation and accountability within the movement**
- **Develop a clear external message for the movement**

As the Council becomes more organized and gains momentum, it intends to periodically share its major ideas and highlights with the public, and will occasionally invite public comment. In balancing efficiency with inclusiveness and transparency, the Council intends to maintain open, clear and transparent communication channels with stakeholders in other organizations, as well as other producer and consumer regions, to collaborate as much as possible.

For more information about the Domestic Fair Trade Organization, please visit
www.thedfta.org

Erin Thompson grew up in the beautiful Puyallup Valley and is currently the Director of food Sovereignty Programs at Community to Community Development. She works with C2C's farmworker leaders on several projects including Cocinas Sanas (Healthy Kitchens), Raices Culturales Bi-lingual Youth mentoring program, the development of CoCoSa- a Culturally Appropriate Cooperative DevelopmentCenter and an organic training farm.

The Château Ste. Michelle Boycott Campaign:
First Labor Contract for the UFW in Washington State since 1972

*Maria Cuevas, Faculty at Yakima Valley Community College
& Community to Community Board Member*

"Organizing [farmworkers] . . . is about transforming the individual to value his or her work and to see the value they have in the whole food system. The transformation is not just with the worker; it is the transformation in the relationships to the land, to the community, to the grower, to other workers. To elevate the farm worker presence in the food production system is how we create and develop leadership and farm worker unity so that they can create the opportunities for change and develop perceptions of why we're here and exist."

—Rosalinda Guillèn, November 2004

Washington State's farmworker history and struggle is not as well known as the history of the southwestern states (particularly California and Texas). With a very different political, social and agro-economic milieu that had effectively worked to keep Latino farmworkers in a vulnerable position, labor organizing in Washington State has presented unique challenges. For example, the social and physical discrimination targeting bracero workers from Mexico during the 1940s often resulted in worker "work stoppages" and strikes to protest the inhumane work conditions typical of the agricultural industry. However, farmworkers were so adept at thwarting the attempts of growers to use migrant workers (from other states and Mexico) against these worker activities that growers eventually gave up and opted to end the Bracero Program in 1947.[1]

The battle to win major labor concessions with Chateau Ste. Michelle (CSM) Wineries took over seven years to accomplish. Begun in the mid- to late 1980's by the workers, they were joined later by community and labor organizers, Tomas

---

1   Gamboa, Erasmo. 2000. *Mexican Labor and World War II: Braceros in the Pacific Northwest, 1942-1947.* Seattle: University of Washington Press.

Villanueva and Lupe Gamboa of Yakima Valley. Problems with management and work conditions (sexual harassment, lack of job security and a grievance process, varying wages and benefits), led the CSM workers to seek help from an independent farmworker organization in Washington State in the late 1980s.

Eventually the successful signing of a labor contract between the United Farm Workers of America, AFL-CIO and the CSM management in December 1995 heralded the first labor contract for the UFW outside of California since 1972 and the most comprehensive and humane contract to benefit farmworkers in Washington State.[2]

Rosalinda Guillèn was brought onto the campaign by the workers in 1991 and by Kurt Peterson, an independent labor advisor to the campaign. Organizing the workers of Château Ste. Michelle Winery, "a tightly knit workforce from Michoacan, Mexico," Rosalinda sought to bring women into the organizing meetings, as they constituted about 30 to 40 percent of the winery workforce. Not accustomed to female leadership, the male workers' "critical consciousness" emerged unplanned as a result of Rosalinda's mentorship and diligence in meting out unfair union practices that subordinated women's roles in the union. By the close of the boycott in late 1994, women and children were a regular part of the union meetings and campaign and eventually equal partners on the job. Moreover, bearing witness to the hard physical and mental work that women were engaging in, resulted in "changes in the way that the men workers related to female workers and to their domestic partners at home."[3]

> "Organizing farm-workers ...is about transforming the individual to value his or her work and to see the value they have in the whole food system."
>
> —Rosalinda Guillèn

After seven plus years of fighting the CSM management, more than 60% of CSM workers voted in a secret ballot to unionize, which surprised many labor experts of the time.[4] The National Labor Relations Act of 1935 does not allow farmworkers to participate in a collective bargaining process with their employer for fair and equal treatment and better working conditions, so the fact

---

2   *According to Rosalinda Guillèn, former National Vice President of the United Farmworker's Union, Sacramento, CA.*

3   *Rosalinda Guillen interview, 2001.*

4   *Jeff Switzer, Northwest News, 1995.*

that workers were allowed to vote was groundbreaking and is the only known labor contract for farmworkers in Washington state (ibid). The contract included a significant pay increase for six job classifications or about 5.5 % wage increase, complete family medical and dental coverage, a pension plan, job security for regular and seasonal workers, a grievance and arbitration procedure, and health and safety rules for protections from pesticides. Additional worker benefits also included meal-time breaks, paid rest periods, paid vacations, and 11 paid holidays (ibid).

Additional unintended benefits are evidenced in the increased profits to the CSM winery[5] in the years following the contract signing, in part due to treating of workers with dignity; workers who believe that they and their work is valued are productive workers.

The success in organizing the Chateau Ste. Michelle workers was a collective effort on the part of the farm workers, the organizers, winery negotiators, and Rosalinda's efforts to maintain a successful collective: performed through the development and maintenance of strong relational networks forged through confrontations of personal beliefs and subsequent actions between the workers and Rosalinda Guillèn's leadership, among the workers, and between the workers and the CSM management.

Maria Cuevas has over 20 years experience working with communities of color, women and youth in popular education, community planning, administration and research. Currently a doctoral candidate at WSU in Pullman, WA, her specialization is in communities and inequality.

---

5   *United Farmworkers Union document on CSM profits, 2001.*

References Cited:
- *Interviews with Rosalinda Guillèn: October 8, 2001; October 14, 2004; November 6 and 7, 2004; November 30, 2004.*
- *Agricultural Workforce in Washington State 2000. prepared by Loretta Payne, Economic and Policy Analysis Unit, Labor Market and Economic Analysis Branch, Washington State Employment Security. August 2001.*
- *Gamboa, Erasmo. 2000. Mexican Labor and World War II: Braceros in the Pacific Northwest, 1942-1947. Seattle: University of Washington Press.*
- *Pascal, Zachary. Wall Street Journal, New York: June 7, 1995.*

A Quick Overview of the Farm Bill

The Northwest Farm Bill Action Group

It's been said that The Farm Bill should be re-named the *Food Bill*, because it influences what we eat every day—from the cost, quality and availability of food, to the tools available to communities to protect farm and ranch land. If we understand the Farm Bill, which has global impacts on food prices and availability, we'll be better able to address the global changes needed to ensure that everyone has access to affordable, healthy food.

What is the Farm Bill?

The Farm Bill is a set of federal laws that establishes the general direction for America's farm and food policy. It is called an "omnibus" bill, which means it covers a broad range of subjects and programs. Congress writes, debates, and passes a new version of the Farm Bill every 5 to 7 years. Some of the programs in the bill are "mandatory" — they are definitely funded, even if they go over-budget, and some are "discretionary," which means Congress assigns funds to pay for them later (or doesn't). The discretionary programs are reviewed every year until a new Farm Bill is written.

What is the History of the Farm Bill?

In 1933 President Franklin D. Roosevelt signed the first farm bill, called the Agricultural Adjustment Act, to aid struggling and increasingly rebellious farmers during the Great Depression. Farmers were faced at the time with rock bottom prices—corn prices actually hit $0! The government began paying "parities," prices roughly equal to what prices should be during favorable market times, for storable crops called "commodities." Farmers were also paid not to produce certain crops, or not to raise livestock; producers were even paid to plow up already planted acres of Southern cotton and large numbers of baby pigs were slaughtered in the Midwest to limit supply and drive up prices.

The first farm bill also addressed national hunger, soil erosion, lack of credit and unfair export practices. Since then, there have been 15 Farm Bills, each with its own name, which have, in one way or another addressed these issues. Unfortunately, many of these original programs, which were designed to ensure that there was enough food for all and fair prices for farmers, have been stripped away or replaced with programs that benefit corporate interests.

What's in the Farm Bill?

The Farm Bill is organized into different areas called "titles." New titles are added as new issues become crucial to the farm economy and movements addressing hunger, environmental preservation and energy. For example, in 2002 a new Energy Title was added to the bill. The current Farm Bill, passed in 2008 is called The Food, Conservation, and Energy Act. It has 15 different titles, including commodity price and income supports, farm credit, trade, food stamps, agricultural conservation, rural development, bio-energy, international food aid and research.

The mandatory spending for the 2008 bill over a period of 5 years was supposed to be about $288 billion. Now it looks like the amount will be closer to $420 billion. This sounds like a huge sum, but is actually less than one percent of the federal budget.

Nutrition programs including the Supplemental Nutrition Assistance Program (SNAP), formerly known as Food Stamps, emergency food assistance, school lunches, the Women, Infant and Children Program (WIC) and the Farmers Market Nutrition Program receive the highest level of funding, 76% of total Farm Bill spending ($314 billion).

> Producers growing fruits and vegetables are not eligible to receive commodity subsidies, so they are more expensive for consumers to buy.
>
> Subsidies influence our choices on the grocery aisle, and therefore our health.

63

Commodity subsidies, the next largest category account for 10% of spending ($32 billion). Commodity Subsidies (money from the government—actually our tax dollars) are paid to farmers growing certain crops—corn, cotton, wheat, rice and soybeans receive the most money. Producers growing fruits and vegetables (called "specialty crops") are not eligible to receive commodity subsidies and so they are more expensive for consumers to buy. Thus, subsidies influence our choices on the grocery aisle, and therefore our health. Importantly, the subsidies also have a large impact on struggling farmers in other countries.

Few people realize that the farm bill is the largest single source of federal funding for conservation on U.S. private land.

In the globalized commodity markets of today, small farmers' crop prices are competing against subsidy-lowered American crop prices. This has devastating consequences. One example: When the North American Free Trade Agreement (NAFTA) opened the doors to agricultural trade with Mexico, subsidized (and therefore cheaper) U.S. corn flooded the Mexican market; many small farmers could not compete and lost their farms. This resulted in the heavy upswing in immigration to the U.S. from Mexico in the 1990s. The disenfranchised corn farmers needed to find work.

Few people realize that the farm bill is the largest single source of federal funding for conservation on U.S. private land—6% of spending ($22 billion). Funding for crop insurance has increased tremendously in recent years; it is now $28 billion.

Who in Congress Writes the Farm Bill?

The House and Senate Agriculture Committees each write their own versions of the bill, and then negotiate the differences. Therefore, the makeup of each committee is critical to how the Farm Bill turns out. Debbie Stabenow (D-Mich.) is the chair of the Senate Agriculture, Nutrition and Forestry Committee, and Frank Lucas (R-OK) is the Chair of the House committee (Lucas is a strong supporter of commodity subsidies, while Stabenow's preferences are less known).

Once passed, the Farm Bill moves into "appropriations"—a process that determines how much money each program receives. In the ultimate paradox, the USDA recommends that we all eat more fruits and vegetables, while the Farm Bill promotes the production of more grain!

An important part of the Farm Bill story is that many worthwhile and publicly-supported programs are vastly under-funded or not funded at all. Programs that would address the need for access to healthy food, organic and sustainable agriculture, community food programs, and support for new farmers and ranchers receive less than 1% of total Farm Bill funding. Also, during the current budget cutting frenzy, the agriculture committees have proposed cutting conservation programs disproportionately more than commodity subsidy and crop insurance programs.

Discussions are well underway in Congress about new legislation for 2012. In the fall of 2011, members of Congress wrote a "Secret" Farm bill for 2012 behind closed doors. Luckily, it was scrapped when the Super Committee failed to reach an agreement on cuts to the federal budget.

The Northwest Farm Bill Action Group is a group of community members who are concerned about the current state of our food system. The organization began organizing under the direction of the Community Alliance for Global Justice in August 2010, after it hosted a community conference called "Food Fight!" which sought to help people understand how the Farm Bill affects them personally and to create a vision for a better Farm Bill.

Today, the Northwest Farm Bill Action Group is building a diverse alliance of people and organizations in the Pacific Northwest who advocate for a more healthy, sustainable, and equitable food system. Through collaboration, we provide a space for Pacific Northwest communities to educate themselves about the upcoming Farm Bill and to cultivate the tools to take action and effect policy change to work for a better food system.

How to get involved

Involve Yourself:

The time for advocating for the changes that we want in the Farm Bill is NOW!

In the Seattle area, get involved through the Northwest Farm Bill Action Group. To join the mailing list, email farmbill@seattleglobaljustice.org. Visit our website: www.nwfoodfight.org and friend us on Facebook.

65

Learn More!

The following groups have published platforms for the 2012 Farm Bill:

- **Community Food Security Coalition:** www.foodsecurity.org/policy

- **Food and Water Watch:** www.foodandwaterwatch.org/food/farm-bill-2012/

- **National Sustainable Agriculture Coalition's 2012 Farm Bill Platform Budget Chapter:** www.sustainableagriculture.net/wp-content/uploads/2011/09

- **The American Farmland Trust** and 55 other groups outlined a set of key principles that law-makers should observe as they write the **Conservation Title** of the 2012 farm bill and seek ways to trim the federal deficit: www.farmland.org/documents/092811JointConservationTitlePrinciples.pdf

The references used to write this piece are listed below and provide an excellent Farm Bill overview:

- Farm Bill 1.01: An Introduction and Brief History of the Farm Bill (Ed Yowell and Fern Gale Estrow, NYC Food Systems Network, 2011). www.foodsystemsnyc.org/articles/farm-bill-jan-2011

- Farm Bill 1.02: The Farm Bill, the Field and the Players (Ed Yowell and Fern Gale Estrow, NYC Food Systems Network, 2011). *Discusses the political players in the 2012 Farm Bill Game and programs that are more vulnerable to being cut.* www.foodsystemsnyc.org/articles/farm-bill-feb-2011

- Farm Bill 1.04: School Lunches and the Farm Bill (Travis Hobart, MD with Fern Gale Estrow, Sheilah Davidson, Thomas Forster, and Ed Yowell, NYC Food Systems Network, June 2011). www.foodsystemsnyc.org/articles/farm-bill-june-2011

- Farm Bill 1.05: H.R. 2112 Defines the 2012 Farm Bill Playing Field (Mark Dunlea with Ed Yowell, NYC Food Systems Network, July 2011) The 2012 Farm Bill Starts with the 2011 Ag Budget. www.foodsystemsnyc.org/articles/farm-bill-july-2011

- Farm Bill 1.06: What You Need to Know about Food Stamps and the 2012 Farm Bill (Michael Crupain MD, MPH with Ed Yowell, August 2011). www.foodsystemsnyc.org/articles/farm-bill-august-2011

- Farm Bill 1.07: The Risky Business of Farming (Abby Youngblood and Ed Yowell, NYC Food Systems Network, October, 2011). *Crop Insurance explained.* www.foodsystemsnyc.org/articles/farm-bill-october-2011

- Top 10 Things You Should Know About The Farm Bill (Sara Sciammacco, Civil Eats, June 30th, 2011). http://civileats.com/2011/06/30/top-10-things-you-should-know-about-the-farm-bill/

- Understanding the Farm Bill: What's Organic Got to Do With It? (Ann Butkowski, Simply Good and Tasty, June 6, 2011). simplegoodandtasty.com/2011/05/31/understanding-the-farm-bill-whats-organic-got-to-do-with-it

- Session on the Farm Bill with Slides (Community Food Security Coalition, February 22, 2011). *To see the slides in PDF format go to:* www.nwfoodfight.org/wp-content/uploads/2012_Farm_Bill-CFSC_Virtual_Listening_Session.pdf

- Organic Farm Bill Policy 101 (Organic Seed Alliance and National Organic Coalition, 2011). www.nwfoodfight.org/wp-content/uploads/Organic-Farm-Bill-Primer.pdf

- Better Food Starts with the Farm Bill (Food & Water Watch, June, 2010). www.nwfoodfight.org/wp-content/uploads/Better-Food-Starts-with-the-Farm-Bill.pdf

- A Farm Bill Primer: Getting Ready for 2012 (Ann Butkowski, Simply Good and Tasty, 2010). http://simplegoodandtasty.com/2010/10/21/a-farm-bill-primer-getting-ready-for-2012

- Actual Farm Bill Spending and Cost Estimates (Jim Monk and Renee Johnson, Congressional Research Service, 2010). www.nationalaglawcenter.org/assets/crs/R41195.pdf

The Just Garden Project.

Who?

Sponsors: Fiscally sponsored by Seattle Tilth.

Funded by: United Way of King County,

Community donations: *Cedar Grove, Cascadian Edible Landscapes, Theo Chocolate, Whole Foods, Ideal Network, Joanne Hill, Skillet, H+dlT, Fremont Brewing, Central Co-op, Here Me!, Homewell Senior Care, and many more!*

What? **Build gardens, educate gardeners, celebrate our local food system, and engage youth to take an active role in this movement.**

When? Build March-May, with four annual celebrations (Launch, Spring into Bed, Fall into Bed, Thanksgiving). Engage year round. Mentor program runs from June–October.

Where? **Seattle and King County. Hopefully soon everywhere!**

Why?? Because we are our thriving local food system. The only way to build a thriving local food system is to build it with and for all people. You are an essential element of this transformation. You make it happen. When you grow healthy food, you can help your neighbors to grow healthy food—it is in this way we create a healthier food system for our future generations.

How: **One garden, gardener, yard, celebration, and youth at a time.**

The Just Garden Project

Stephanie Seliga-Soulseed, Founder & Director of The Just Garden Project

The roar of the freeway echoes in the background as we pull the dewy blue tarp from planks of re-claimed wood. The Just Garden Project's dedicated interns move quickly and quietly, filling the van with 18 eight-foot planks. We close the door on the borrowed van before driving to where the tools are stored.

Three volunteers are waiting as we turn the corner to the parking lot behind GroundUp Organics—a community organization engaging youth of color in the green movement. Just Garden Volunteers, interns, and staff join the GroundUp Crew, forming a circle. We go around, each person saying his or her name and favorite memory about food. Memories of Thanksgiving dinners, homemade cinnamon buns, and someone mistaking the wasabi for avocado help us connect and find common ground for the task at hand—building two new backyard gardens for families in King County.

> We connect and find common ground for the task at hand—building two new backyard gardens for families in King County.

Building a just food system and a culture of gardening for all people is the mission of the Just Garden Project. We do this work by bringing together local resources, businesses, communities and individuals within King County. In 2011, the Just Garden Project built 33 gardens, organized over 300 volunteers, and tallied over 3,500 volunteer hours in just six months.

Each of these gardens has the potential of producing upwards of $650 worth of organic fruits and vegetables. As the costs of gas, food, and living go up, these gardens offer hope and real sustenance for people struggling to make ends meet. The JGP exists in the space created by decades of dedicated garden work in Seattle. Resources from the city's compost system fill the gardens with soil. An existing program giving free seeds to gardeners who want to grow for the food bank provides bags of regionally appropriate seeds for each of our gardeners. Donors and volunteers are the glue that holds the program together. Donations come in from local businesses and individuals funding the work and giving the Just Garden Project the community support we need to keep our work going. Volunteers do everything from sending out thank-you notes to physically building gardens. Together our donors and volunteers are the motor behind the magic.

We pull up to the small house. The gardeners are waiting on the porch for us. People arrive in cars and on bikes. Before we know it, 13 people have amassed to do the work of four. We work together, socialize and enjoy ourselves. One crew digs out the sod, another nails the boards together, another begins moving the soil to the first complete bed. Within two hours we have built three new raised beds, and some new community. At this site, the family has a snack and tea for us when we're done.

It's simple and profound. Gardens offer more than just food. They feed people faith, love, hope, and charity.

The whole team and family circle up on the porch. Like we began the morning, we go around, say our names one more time and our favorite memory of the day. People reflect on how easy it is to build a garden, how nice it is to meet a neighbor, the ease with which we all worked together, how cool it is to do work and see immediate result. We toast with our tea, give hugs, and go to the next garden of the day.

It's simple and profound. Gardens offer more than just food. They feed people faith, love, hope, and charity. Together, we are proving that we *can* create a secure local foodshed. We *can* build a fair and just local food system. Our children and future generations *will* grow up with a connection to where their food comes from. We *are* willing to do what it takes to make our community healthy and edible for everyone from *all* different social, cultural, and economic backgrounds!

Stephanie Seliga-Soulseed is the founder and Director of the Just Garden Project. She lives with her husband Michael Seliga-Soulseed in Seattle, Washington, USA, where they enjoy good food, good people and the everyday practice of walking in balance in a good way.

Sustainable Food Education at the Seattle Culinary Academy

Vicki Briggs

Seattle Culinary Academy (SCA) offers a culinary education that extends well beyond the walls of the kitchen. This unique and much-needed curriculum incorporates questions about how and why SCA students and graduates can make choices that support more sustainable food systems. While learning the required basics like accurate knife skills, perfect preparation of sauces and stocks, and restaurant management, they are also gaining an understanding of how their purchasing choices affect the ecological, economic, and social systems to which they are connected. The school's mission statement says it simply: "commitment to practices that respect heritage, the process, and the health of the planet for future generations."

Since 2005, SCA has offered more and more sustainability courses geared specifically for its culinary students. Now, throughout their 18-month program, students will take three one-credit classes on sustainable food system practices taught by several of their chef instructors.

This series of classes begins with a discussion about what a sustainable food system really looks like. Students learn about genetically modified ingredients and problems with labeling of food products. Later, students focus on animal husbandry practices and sustainable fisheries, exploring what is healthy for the planet, the animals, and diners. They also develop seasonal local menus. Finally, the program addresses issues of food sovereignty, food justice, and food politics.

Speakers from different local organizations explain their work, and students develop a connection for their own volunteer hours following graduation, through a local non-profit research project.

In addition to these dedicated courses, other SCA classes have incorporated sustainability issues into their curricula. Costing and purchasing classes discuss buying from local producers, while management classes include how to promote support of the local food community and how to ensure it benefits the student's future food business.

Students apply this learning about sustainable food models outside of the classroom as well. The school operates a bistro-style café, a fine dining restaurant, and a pastry case. "One World," the fine dining restaurant at Seattle Central Community College, is run by Chef Instructor Kären Jurgenson and her 4th-quarter students. The kitchen is completely GMO-free with a transition to organic canola oil in the deep fryer and elimination of any potential GMO-containing food products. The specialty desserts and baking program uses organic flours and fair trade chocolate in the bakeshop. Students practice in-season food preservation through techniques like canning, curing, and pickling.

> While learning the required basics like accurate knife skills, students also gain an understanding of how their choices affect the ecological, economic, and social systems to which they are connected.

A unique summer learning program offers students the opportunity to visit La Conner Flats Farm in the Skagit Valley each week and return with produce to use on the menu. This "Seed-to-Plate Education" involves planting, maintaining, harvesting, preparing, and serving local produce. Additionally, students visit other types of farms during the weekly trips, including Skagit River Ranch for beef & poultry and the well-known Taylor Shellfish Farm, making connections to growers and producers who are contributing to the revitalization of a local, sustainable food system.

Bringing the "urban farming" concept close to home, in the spring 2011 quarter, the Plant Science Lab—a.k.a. the Greenhouse—opened on campus, bringing the "urban farming" concept close to home. Lettuces, herbs, and flowers are grown for use in the school's restaurant dining rooms. Students also have a one-credit class rotation in the greenhouse to learn basics of urban gardening and how to bring the freshest possible ingredients into the kitchen.

After 18 months of study and practice, students complete their degrees at Seattle Culinary Academy. These future chefs, restaurant managers, cooks, and bakers graduate not only with a culinary degree, but also with a sustainability-focused food education that equips them with the knowledge of how, and why they would want to, use their skills to foster human and environmental well-being.

For more information on the program, please visit:
www.seattlecentral.edu/seattleculinary/

Vicki Briggs graduated from the Seattle Culinary Academy in 2011. She lives in Detroit, Michigan where she enjoys discovering the local farmers markets and small town coffee shops. She loves to talk about food, cook with coworkers and friends, and plans to learn a little gardening this summer!

Yardsharing:
how to grow a garden, support food justice, and be a good neighbor, all from your own backyard

Peter Rothbart, founder of We Patch, the online yardsharing program

Rising food prices along with burgeoning interest in sustainable agriculture, food sovereignty, and the slow food movement have created a boom in gardening efforts nationwide. Seattle's P-Patch Community Gardening Program, for example, provides gardening and recreational space to over 4,400 community gardeners, with 75 gardens spread across 23 acres throughout the city. In 2010, P-Patch gardeners responded by supplying nearly 21,000 pounds of fresh produce to local food banks and, with other community members, donating 17,000 hours of labor to maintaining common areas. (Statistics taken from the P-Patch page at the City of Seattle website)

Yet, as much as the P-Patch program, which is managed by the city's Department of Neighborhoods, is a testament to the value of public services, it also exemplifies their limitations. Space is in short supply and high demand, as waiting lists for many P-Patches remain years long. Plot sizes are kept small to accommodate as many gardeners as possible, so that even those who are offered land may find their allotted spaces insufficient. This problem is not unique to Seattle, as the growing popularity of community gardening has intensified the need for space in many urban areas. In response, some gardeners have begun to seek other solutions.

One such solution is **yardsharing**, a new variety of community gardening in which people create garden space from the abundant, and otherwise idle, land in their neighborhood—most notably, their neighbors' yards.

Yardsharing arrangements are simple, but powerful. One individual looking for land, called a planter, joins forces with a partner who has land to spare. Planters offer to cultivate and tend the land, while partners offer the use of their yards in exchange for some of the produce. The foremost benefit is that yardsharing helps people produce their own food; however, yardsharing has other less tangible benefits that are equally important.

First, yardsharing promotes food sovereignty and environmental stewardship by empowering individuals to retake control over their means of food production. In a global food system that caters to increasingly monolithic corporations, growing one's own food is a potent equalizer.

Food grown by consumers bypasses the industrial food system that often supports unfair labor practices and unsustainable global food policies. Furthermore, those who grow their own food get to dictate the terms on which it is grown—for example, whether organic or GMO varieties are used, whether pesticides or chemical fertilizers are used, and how water resources are managed. Unlike store-bought food, gardeners know they can trust that produce picked from their own garden is organic and fair-wage, because they planted it, nurtured it, and harvested it.

Second, yardsharing promotes a slow food culture by rejecting the "bigger, cheaper, and faster" mantra of the industrial food system. When the goal is only to maximize the dispensation and consumption of calories, then where our food comes from and why we eat it in the first place are secondary. Yardsharing (and gardening in general) reinvigorates the notion that food should sustain us holistically by nourishing our spirits as well as our bodies.

Finally, yardsharing strengthens local communities by turning strangers into neighbors. One trend in modern, particularly urban, society is the loss of community identity that has attended the increased mobility of the automobile culture and the ubiquity of cell phones and the internet. Americans have disengaged *en masse* from direct social interaction with neighbors: fewer than half of Americans

Yardsharing counteracts urban anonymity by fostering interactions between planters & partners, encouraging people to meet others in their communities face-to-face where the spade meets the dirt.

75

report talking personally with neighbors about community issues, and nearly 60 percent report that they do not know their neighbors by name, according to the Pew Research Center. Yardsharing counteracts this by fostering interactions and emphasizing cooperation between planters and partners, encouraging people to meet others in their communities face to face where the spade meets the dirt, and to make their neighborhoods more familiar places by doing so.

A number of organizations now exist to facilitate yardsharing by connecting people looking for garden space with those who have space to offer. Web-based services such as *We Patch*, *Yards to Gardens*, and others listed below, enable users to quickly and easily establish yardsharing agreements in their own neighborhoods. While most services offer guidelines, such as a recommended split of the produce, users are encouraged to develop their own agreements that work for them. Some services are specific to one city or region, while others are offered nationwide or internationally. All of the services listed are free and run by volunteers. Those interested in yardsharing should visit each site and determine which service suits them best.

Whether you're an apartment dweller in search of your own vegetable plot or a homeowner with extra land and not enough time to tend it, yardsharing is a compelling and viable new option. The more people using yardsharing programs like those mentioned in this article, the more useful such programs will be to everyone. Look for opportunities in your area and find new ways to grow!

Interested in yardsharing? These organizations can help you get started!

We Patch (USA)
www.wepatch.org

Landshare (UK)
www.landshare.net

Yardsharing (Portland, OR)
www.yardsharing.org

Neighborhood Fruit (USA)
www.neighborhoodfruit.com

Yards to Gardens (Minneapolis)
www.y2g.org

Peter Rothbart is the director of the yardsharing organization We Patch and an editor at FOUND Magazine. He lives in Seattle.

The Washington Young Farmers Coalition Cultivates Community

Addie Candib

Eaters everywhere are beginning to notice that our food systems are in a state of disrepair. From depleted soils and pesticide build-up, fossil fuel dependence and aging farmers to rampant obesity, other food-related illness and rising costs and falling incomes, the national outlook is bleak.

A lot needs to be changed to re-envision and rebuild our food systems, but first and foremost, we need more farmers. The oft-cited number for the average age of farmers in the U.S.—57—looms large in our food future. However, numbers of young people are turning to agriculture as a livelihood and a way to make meaningful change. But the Homestead Act expired in 1976; starting a farm is no longer as simple as staking a claim and improving the land. For young people not born into agricultural families, gaining access to land to farm in this era of exorbitant property values and reluctant lenders can pose quite a challenge.

And access to land is really just the first hurdle. The ingredients necessary to grow a successful young farmer are many and variable. Even the most bound and determined young person will still need access to land, financial resources, proximity to markets, education and mentorship, ongoing skill-sharing and development, agriculture-friendly policy at the state and federal levels, and perhaps, most important, a robust and supportive community.

It was with that list of needs in mind that, in October of 2010, a handful of young farmers in Washington State, some of them managing their own farms, others apprenticing for an older generation, threw a party. Over 200 people attended the "First Annual Young Farmers Mixer" on Vashon Island. The air positively thrummed with excitement as farmers and farmers' friends from throughout the region crowded a small grange hall to eat, laugh, and dance, marking the birth of the Washington Young Farmers Coalition.

77

A grassroots group for and of the young farmers of Washington State, the Coalition now exists to support Washington's beginning farmers in creating a vital statewide agrarian revival by offering unique social and educational events, enabling access to critical resources, and fostering a strong community of allies.

The Coalition supports beginning farmers in creating a vital state-wide agrarian revival by offering unique events, enabling access to resources, and fostering a strong community of allies.

The energy and exuberance generated by the 2010 mixer continue. Since then, WAYFC has worked to build relationships with other compatible local and national organizations, including the National Young Farmers Coalition, to promote access to farmland, organize financial support for beginning growers, and leverage the voice of young farmers to effect change at the policy level. A few of the more tech-savvy Coalition members are developing a web-based skills matrix to better enable farmers to share knowledge and resources. The Coalition has sponsored a number of small workshops and "crop mobs" (work parties), and more mixers.

Above and beyond its organizing efforts, the most important effects of the Washington Young Farmers Coalition are the creation of intrinsic community and support networks. Meetings, crop mobs, and mixers offer chances for far-flung friends to check in and compare notes, opportunities for new farmers to connect with mentors, and, for many, much-needed reprieves from the daily agricultural grind.

The nature of farming life can be both exhausting and isolating. During the busiest times of year, many farmers won't leave the fields save to eat and sleep—if that! Some young farmers live in rural areas where they are the only organic farmers, or the only young farmers; some start their livelihoods in neighborhoods where they are the only farmers. Ongoing success for these beginning farmers will depend on sustainability, not just of their farms, but of their lifestyles as well. The up-and-coming generation of growers needs a coherent community of allies to support, encourage, and validate their work. The Washington Young Farmers Coalition is rising to meet that demand, reminding us that the work of growing food and changing food systems is a shared project, and we are very much in it together.

Connect with the Coalition online at: www.washingtonyoungfarmers.org

Addie Candib lives in Olympia, WA where she grows veggies, saves seed, raises pigs, and works to build community with her fellow farmers.

The Wider Movement: The Greenhorns

GREENHORNS

"The news is in from urban, suburban and rural districts alike: America wants more young farmers and more young farmers want a piece of America. We know it will take millions of these rough and ready protagonists of place to care for our ecosystems and serve our country healthy food in the years to come. The Greenhorns enable this critical meeting between minds, bodies, and land by helping young and aspiring farmers to navigate career paths, build skills, and connect with each other. Our multifaceted approach includes on-the-ground organizing of events and workshops, media production, and online coalition building.

"The Greenhorns, founded in 2007, is a grassroots non-profit organization made up of young farmers and many collaborators. Our mission is to recruit, promote and support the new generation of young farmers in this ample and able 21st century America. The Greenhorns team is widespread and volunteer-driven. Projects are initiated under the leadership of the director and other senior members, and are frequently inspired by feedback from our constituency of young farmers.

"We think our organizational model is particularly effective for nimble national grassroots work on a modest budget. Together we act as a cultural 'meme' that creates positive rhetoric, messaging, materials, and procedures that are replicable and adaptable. Thus our network continues to branch out and take on diverse local facets."

Connect with the Greenhorns online at: www.thegreenhorns.net

All information, with permission, from the Greenhorns' website. Graphic by Brooke Budner.

To meet a local leader in the Washington Young Farmers Coalition, see the Farmer Profile of Chandler Briggs on the very first page of the next section.

The Harvest   *Joanna Wright*

Here, another harvest day begins:
blink away sleep, step
barefoot in the cold grass toward open arms
of a deep, glowing sunrise.

In this field of simplicity
and abundance
   look! Swollen corn,
   tomatoes tugging on their vines,
   canteloupe too sweet at the bellybutton
my hands move in a steady sign language,
speaking gratitude, and wonder.

Even after too many of our
human ambitions
have scarred the earth with carelessness,
for the moment, she
continues to forgive.
This ridiculous bounty of summer has come
again
despite our grand failure to love the
soil
water
air
as we love ourselves.

Amidst this confusion, there is
perhaps
a small grace. I saw
our four-year-old whisper
to the worms today, watched
her smile grow as one wiggled across her open
palm,
dangled like a question between her fingers.

The sunlight
harvested my heartbeat
asking nothing in
return.

Farmer Profiles

Food Justice Project member Joanna Wright sought out leaders in the world of Pacific Northwest farming, both young and seasoned, to pick their brains about the joys and trials of urban and rural farms, the role of a farm in its community, and the challenges of growing food in the 21st century.

Photos this section courtesy of the farms and farmers.

Farmer Profile

Chandler Briggs, Island Meadow Farm, Vashon Island, WA

Chandler Briggs, a Southern California native, has been farming vegetables, fruit, flowers, and livestock for over five years. Pictured here at Island Meadow Farm on Vashon Island, he also organizes with the Washington Young Farmers Coalition and Cascade Harvest Coalition.

How would you describe your farm?

For the last three years, I've been managing Island Meadow, a small bio-diverse farm on Vashon Island. I came to the farm excited to carry on its rich legacy, a decades-long history of providing nutritious, delicious food to the surrounding community, from their start at the Pike Place Market, to our farm stand, farmer's market and direct to restaurant sales today. As a beginning and young farmer, I was able to step into this (nearly) turn-key operation and gain skills running a successful farm business while acquiring mobile capital. It was an ideal step after spending a few years apprenticing on other similar small family farms.

For the 2012 season, I will be leaving the farm in pursuit of horsedrawn farming by apprenticing with Welcome Table Farm in Walla Walla. In this endeavor, I hope to broaden my farming skill set, working under Andy Asmus and Emily Dietzman with their team of American Belgians.

Whether at Island Meadow or elsewhere, I seek to farm in an ecologically and socially responsible way, which cultivates a diverse ecology and produces fresh healthy food. I want to feed myself and my community, while leaving the place in better shape than I found it. I also seek to participate in the farmer networks to encourage and support innovation, sharing and agrarian camaraderie.

What are the main challenges you face?

As a young entrepreneur with no childhood background in rural living, let alone farming, I am facing an uphill battle in my farming career. I do not have a legacy of ancestors who might pass down knowledge, equipment and land, as was the case in many previous generations. I don't have the years of a childhood farm life to draw upon for wisdom. But while I lack experience, I have energy and enthusiasm. I also have a growing market of excited consumers looking to feed themselves and their families with wholesome food.

Like the challenges many young farmers face, as reported by the National Young Farmers Coalition in their 2011 report, "Building a Future with Farmers," I need access to land, capital and affordable health insurance. Farming is a strenuous job, financially, physically and mentally, and in order to succeed, farmers deserve to be paid fairly and receive help when we get sick or hurt. If we as a society value small farmers, we need the actions to back up the claims.

How might the community support you in addressing these challenges?

The problems we face both as a society and a smaller community of farmers are multifaceted, complicated and overwhelming. From lack of health care, unequal dispersion of wealth, to peak everything, we face a long road ahead—there are no easy answers. I believe our society will need to face radical lifestyle changes before we see solutions to the deeply rooted problems. The real shift in our food system (and by association, solutions to challenges farmers like myself face) will come when we stop sweeping externalities under the rug and truly confront problems, like our government's favorability of industrial agribusiness, our culture's obsession with material wealth over quality food and our country's fixation on policing the world with the monstrous military.

The most I can ask from my immediate, regional community is support—financially, physically, politically. Spending your hard-earned dollars with responsible local producers encourages farmers to continue growing; participating in the growing of your own food develops thoughtful, healthy consumers, and remaining engaged in important political choices keeps our government in check and

Read the National Young Farmers Coalition report, "Building a Future with Farmers" from Oct. 2011 at:

www.youngfarmers.org

working for us. I ask that everyone pay attention to the Farm Bill—it has a big impact on the world of agriculture, from small farmers to corporate agribusiness.

What accomplishments are you most proud of?

Embracing pride doesn't suit me well—but I'll admit that I am lucky to have the privilege of following my dreams by living and working on farms, in constant pursuit of being a better farmer. I am so delighted that I have the support from friends, family and others in my community to do what I love by feeding people.

What is important to you about the role that your farm plays in your community?

Growing high-quality, delicious, nutrient-dense food for my neighbors means seeing my customers at the store or coffee shop and being accountable by being present within the community. And it's important to participate in activism that supports other small and beginning farmers.

See the fruits of Chandler's and many other young farmers' activism in "Washington Young Farmers Coalition Cultivates Community," p. 77

Chandler Briggs, a 28-year-old Southern California native, gave up a life in the sand for one in the soil. He has been farming vegetables, fruit, flowers, and livestock for over five years. An aspiring teamster, he is apprenticing on a draft horse-powered farm before setting out on his own horse-powered farm. He also organizes with the Washington Young Farmers Coalition and Cascade Harvest Coalition.

Farmer Profile

Lottie Cross, Director, Clean Greens Farm & Market, Seattle & Duvall, WA

Lottie Cross is the Director of Clean Greens Farm & Market. Clean Greens was founded in 2007 to educate citizens and produce buyers in healthy eating and food justice, and to supply fresh, wholesome produce to families in need in Seattle's Central District and other communities.

How would you describe your project?

We describe Clean Greens Farm and Market as a project to provide low income people a means to eat healthy produce that they are accustomed to primarily from the southern states, such as collard, mustard and turnips greens, as well as some produce they are not accustomed to, at a price they can afford. It is a project that brings people together to learn how to plant, pull weeds, watch the produce grow and the work that goes into bringing the produce to harvest and to the market. And it is a project to produce food while educating the youth as well as the old on how important it is to eat healthily.

What are the main challenges you face?

Our largest challenge over the five years is lack of funds, which makes it very difficult to buy the equipment we need to develop the farm in a timely manner each year and the way we want to advance it to serve more people. Most times we have to wait until other farmers finish working their farms, then they come over to help us, which puts us behind. There's a lack of funds to hire or pay the farmers we have. We are thankful that a lot of the work is volunteered. It amazes me sometimes how we do so much with so little. But we have a lot of good people that keep us going with their volunteer hours.

How might the community support you in addressing these challenges?

The community can help by supporting the market, getting the word out to everyone by going door to door with flyers, donating items such as hoes, gloves and bags, manning the markets, being a volunteer coordinator and a CSA coordinator. We need lots of volunteers to go to the farm when it's time to plant, and at weeding and harvest time. It would be good to have a grant writer to research and write & track grants.

What accomplishments are you most proud of?

We are most proud of all the partnerships we had made such as working with CAGJ, Central Co-op, Holy Cross Episcopal Church, Odessa Brown Community Kitchen, Damascus Baptist Church, UFCW Local 21, Earth Ministries, and St Marks Episcopal Church. We are proud of the many volunteers that have helped us, many of them whom were from the University of Washington, and the many CSA members that we have had over the years. If it had not been for them, Clean Greens would have failed.

There are so many accomplishments, but the last two I will mention is the Fork & Frames Bicycle group that came in and recruited their own CSA members and delivered boxes to them every week by bicycle, and our Giveaway program. We gave over 20,000 pounds of produce to four food banks this year. We are very proud to be able to give. We also donated produce to the Odessa Brown Community Kitchen.

What is important to you about the role that you play in your community?

It is important to me that the community is so happy that they have a market in the Central Area of Seattle where they can buy fresh and healthy produce each week. Each year more and more people are learning about the market. We have people coming from as far as Shoreline and Federal Way to get to our market.

They like the fact that our bunches of greens are big and fresh straight from the farm for the low price. We have a lot of young people helping us at the market and they love it. Another important part of our market is now we can accept EBT cards & WIC. We also accept visa & mastercard.

To learn more about Clean Greens, read "Lentils and Justice for All," a Yes! Magazine interview with Clean Greens founder Rev. Jeffrey and Brahm Ahmadi, co-founder of Oakland based People's Grocery:

yesmagazine.org/peace-justice/lentils-and-justice-for-all-1

Founded in 2007 by Rev. Robert L. Jeffrey, Sr., Clean Greens Farm and Market was established to educate citizens and produce buyers in healthy eating and food justice, and to supply fresh, wholesome produce to families in need in Seattle's Central District and other communities. Clean Greens offers affordable produce through their CSA (Community Supported Agriculture) program. This program enables residents to purchase fresh produce directly from their local farm, located in Duvall, WA, 25 miles outside of Seattle.

Get involved at: www.cleangreensfarm.com

Farmer Profile
Sue McGann, Marra Farm, Seattle WA

Sue McGann is Lettuce Link's Coordinator at Marra Farm, a model urban community farm engaging people in sustainable agriculture and education while enhancing local food security. Sue coordinates the Giving Garden, which generates tons of fresh, organic produce every year that is donated to local food banks.

How would you describe Marra Farm? What are the goals and how do you work toward them?

Marra Farm is a community farm, so there are a few different organizations working here. We have a P-Patch that represents 25 families, the Mien community garden with around 20 families, the Lettuce Link Giving Garden, and of course, all the work that's done here is done by volunteers and the produce goes to the food bank in South Park.

Also part of our program is the Children's Garden, as well as a partnership with the Head Start program, and we just started a small CSA this year to bring some money in for our programs. We also just started a Community Kitchen program, working with Lettuce Link, SeaMar, the Community Center and the nutrition students from Bastyr University. There was a group of people who got together, cooked together and had a nutrition lesson, and ate together, and also brought food home; it was hugely successful.

This [South Park] is a community with no grocery store, terrible transportation, and a lot of immigrants who are working two to three jobs and are totally stressed out, and children, who have growing brains that can't grow if they don't get fruits and vegetables. So I think it's really important in any community, where there are children, especially, to take care of those brains so that they can take care of our world when they get old enough.

In a just world, we would not need food banks, except maybe for a catastrophe from nature, but we are not in a just world, so we have to do two different things: we have to make a just world, and we have to make a safety net for all the people who are treated unjustly.

What are the main challenges that Marra Farm faces?

I think the biggest challenge right now is really keeping the community engaged. I think this community is a representation of most communities in the sense that there is a section of the community who are activists and other people are getting by or doing their own thing. Many people in this community are illegal immigrants, and don't want to be anywhere that draws attention to them, or they're working multiple jobs and are just too busy.

I think that, as times get harder, people will become more engaged down here. This year I actually have a whole handful of volunteers, young people who live in this community who've been volunteering. It's about…educating people about things that they need to know, so that when hard times come, they can be resilient.

The other main challenge is funding to do the work that we do down here. It all costs money, and funding is always a struggle.

How might the community support you in addressing these challenges?

I would say the help with funding, through partnerships with other businesses and organizations, is really valuable. Also, volunteering! Lettuce Link is like CAGJ, it's completely volunteer-driven. It's a win-win situation; people love to volunteer, it makes them feel good, it makes the people who they're working with feel good, and it helps out the organization. So the volunteer's effort down here is huge.

What accomplishments are you most proud of?

I think I really like the kids' garden the best. It has really taken off; we have several classes from Concord Elementary that come regularly during the school year, and the garden curriculum has gotten really, really good. It's super science based, and the kids get to design their own experiments. They get to ask: What would happen if…?

We have a summer camp where kids come during the summer, and now the Head Start program as well. If we're going to actually change people's eating habits and their thinking about things, we have to start with children.

Kids are so often not engaged in nature these days. And here we have climate change impacting things all over the world, and how are we going to deal with it if these kids grow up without being connected to nature in any way? If they don't have a relationship with nature, then they won't care about it. So we have to engage kids in nature, and they want to; they're so excited when they see bugs and worms and spiders and…real life!

It's also interesting because a lot of these kids are poor. So if they come down here with brand new shoes on, that they just got, they don't want to get them dirty. They don't want to get them dirty for two reasons. One is that they're poor and these are brand new shoes, and because they don't want to get anything dirty because they don't' have any relationship with dirt. As soon as we show them how fun it is to get dirty, then it's okay. But sometimes we have to encourage them to get a little dirty.

How have you been impacted, in positive or negative ways, by the Farm Bill?

I don't think we've been impacted by the Farm Bill directly, because that's geared towards Big Ag… But we have, actually, because the money should be coming here instead of going to Cargill!

For all the volunteers who come through here, they first circle up and I give them a talk about the farm, history of the farm, and agriculture—what's happened,

what it means to small family farmers, and going into the 2008 Farm Bill I passed out literature on it and asked people to get involved, and people did, in many ways. And we're doing it again, because now we're on the Farm Bill again.
In that way, the Farm Bill has impacted me, because if it wasn't such a horrific piece of legislation, I wouldn't be bothered with it. We have to educate people about it…most people don't know about it.

What is important to you about the role that your farm plays in your community?

To make sure that there's a safety net for people that need a safety net. This whole farm is really a safety net for this community; when times get hard, they have this land that they can grow food on and they will have educated children that know how to do that.

To learn more about the Farm Bill, see "Farm Bill Overview" from the Northwest Farm Bill Action Group on p. 62

Sue McGann is a Master Gardener, creative community activist, permaculture practitioner and educator. She is a steering committee leader on the Urban Farmer and Awareness guilds of Sustainable NE Seattle, working to build resilience within her neighborhood.

Farmer Profile

Jason Salvo and Siri Erickson-Brown, Local Roots Farm, Duvall WA

Local Roots Farm is a 10-acre diversified vegetable farm located in the Snoqualmie Valley, 20 miles East of Seattle. Jason and Siri founded Local Roots Farm in 2007 and have been selling produce through their CSA subscription program, at Seattle-area farmers markets, and to the region's best restaurants ever since.

How would you describe your farm?

We own and operate Local Roots Farm, an eight-acre diversified vegetable farm near Duvall, WA. We sell vegetables through our CSA subscription program, at two Seattle-area farmers markets, and to many Seattle-area restaurants.

What are the main challenges you face?

The challenges we face are many. From floods, wet weather, dry weather, hot weather, cold weather, farming is fraught with weather-related uncertainty. Luckily, growing a wide diversity of crops is a hedge against the vagaries of the weather. Beyond weather related challenges, right now, the challenge at the forefront of our minds is how to appropriately scale our farm. We want to be big enough that we can afford to pay our workers a living wage but small enough that the work we do every day can still be called farming.

How might the community support you in addressing these challenges?

For a small farm like ours, community support is our lifeblood. From our Community Supported Agriculture subscription program, which brings in much needed income before growing season begins, to our farmers market customers and the restaurants we work with, nearly every vegetable we sell is to someone we know. The community in the Seattle area could support us and our fellow small farmers by getting better educated about the many policy issues that we face trying to farm in a highly urbanized county, where farmland is scarce and expensive.

What accomplishments are you most proud of?

After farming our first four years on leased ground, we lost our lease at the end of 2010. Not long after we received that devastating news, we learned of a 40-acre farm for sale not far from our old farm. With a newborn baby in tow, this past growing season we navigated the purchase of our new farm, grew eight acres of vegetables there, and had the best season we've ever had.

What is important to you about the role that your farm plays in your community?

Beyond providing healthy and nourishing food for our community, another role we have for our farm is that of an experiment. There is a lot of lip service paid to small-scale, organic, agriculture being the antidote to the ills of large-scale corporate agriculture. But the challenges for this new breed of farm are many. In essence, we are trying to answer the question whether our breed of farm can be socially, environmentally, and financially sustainable.

Farmer Profile

Erick and Wendy Haakenson, Jubilee Biodynamic Farm, Carnation WA

Erick and Wendy Haakenson own and manage Jubilee Biodynamic Farm in Carnation, WA, the second CSA (Community Supported Agriculture) farm in Washington State. Here we speak with Erick, a philosopher and theologian, also teaches philosophy at Bellevue College.

How would you describe your farm?

We began farming here at Jubilee Farm in 1989. It's been a long and at times convoluted path that has lead to where we are today. To say we knew nothing about farming when we started is almost an overstatement; we were naïve as the day is long. Moreover, we didn't really exactly know why we had even "bought the farm," or what we were going to do with it.

We learned through practice. Certainly there have been many "cerebral" breakthroughs along the way, but by and large, time and again, it was in doing that we learned what we needed to do, and how to do it. The same, for us, was true of the ideology of the agrarian lifestyle to which we were unknowingly being drawn. For us, and I think this is true of many others as well, farming plowed the barren soil of our hearts, our minds, and our souls.

As the practice of farming accomplished its work, and to the degree to which that work has been accomplished, a vision of our "project" has emerged. We have come to believe that whereas there are many relative goals—sub-goals if you will—that an organic/sustainable farmer can set, there is really one ultimate goal and demand of sustainable farming, and that is to eliminate off-farm inputs. Although we are light years from attaining this goal, we nevertheless hold that vision before us and have taken some steps we believe to be leading us in the right direction.

The first step is in the area of fertility. Can a farm really produce both crops and enough fertility to return to the fields to produce crops for the subsequent season? Can this be done without bringing in that fertility from some other place, and thereby depriving that place of its fertility?

We have come to believe it can be done, but only by conscientiously and mindfully working with natural processes to convert and store the solar energy that is available to every farmer. That's done by allowing that energy to be converted into grass, which is eaten by ruminants, therein being transformed both to sustenance for us, and fertility for the fields. The sun truly is, as Plato said thousands of years ago, "a dispensation, as it were, of grace, that provides the existence of everything in the visible world."

A second step has been trying to reclaim the simple agrarian dignity of managing our own seed stock. Hybrid "vigor," though tantalizing, is a one-year phenomenon; true sustainability calls for the stewardship of careful observation, selection, and preservation of open pollinated, non-proprietary seeds. Here too we have a long way to go. But we are making gains.

A third step has been the recognition that it would require many like-minded people to achieve the goals we've set. By involving up to a hundred such people in a substantial way on the farm each year we have harvested a great deal of synergistic energy: these people have helped to sustain the farm, and the farm has helped to sustain them. The recognition that the source of our food is also a center of the life of the community is an essential contributor to the vital force that transforms mere dirt into soil, and autonomous individuals into a family.

What are the main challenges you face?

Our economic system, to quote Lester Brown, has institutionalized the "art of lying about the true costs of commodities." Although we are surrounded by a supportive community, both we and the members of this community are constantly bombarded by marketers who make their way by externalizing costs. Hence we are assaulted daily by prices that fail to reflect the true environmental, health, and social costs of the goods that are trafficked as commodities, and our food as well.

95

I guess it's no different than it's always been. People of conscience can't/won't take the path most commonly travelled, and going the other way is sometimes just plain wearisome. The main challenge I face is to just "keep the faith." Most producers and consumers willfully ignore the subject of externalized costs, in the same way that our politicians ignore the subject of deficits and deficit spending.

We all know the day of accounting is only being delayed. But waiting is hard. I hear the voice of the earth whose fertility is being depleted, I hear the voices of people whose health and vitality is being lost through poor nutrition and nutrition-related diseases, I hear the voice of the environment that is being ravaged without hesitation to prolong (for a short time) our consumptive ways, and more than all the other voices, I hear the voice of the untold millions of people, some close to home, many far away, whose labor, resources, and right to the pursuit of happiness is being forfeited for the sake of a consumptive minority.

How might the community support you in addressing these challenges?

We live in a progressive region of a progressive state. I believe we who farm responsibly in this area receive a tremendous amount of support. But there is something that just came to mind as I thought about this question.

What if people in Seattle, the tens of thousands (or more?) who genuinely and enthusiastically support local, sustainable agriculture—what if these people started a "eat organic/sustainable" campaign that would ask people to commit (sign up) to eat only foods that are grown organically/sustainably, and when possible, locally, for a year? It would be kind of a boycott of all agri/business, commodity, GMO, processed food that would be organized to the point that we could keep track and have a list (to tally the total number) of people who have signed on. That would be very supportive to me as I face the challenges mentioned above.

And, who knows? It just might catch on, and start something. The time could be right, right now, and if not, the time will soon come. The "occupy" movement has demonstrated there are many people who want change and are willing to take a stand. When will we find the vehicle to take a united economic stand that will bring down those who care for neither the health of the earth and well-being of humanity, or for the virtual servitude of the poor in other countries that helps support our privilege and affluence?

What accomplishments are you most proud of?

I'm proud that for once in my life I've followed both my mind and my heart to engage the path of sustainability for this farm, wherever it leads. Beyond that, standing with fellow farmers in a lawsuit against the Army Corps of Engineers, spreading 100,000 pounds of compost on fallow fields last year, being allowed by Sno-Valley Tilth to lead the mentoring program for new farmers in our valley, and proving all the skeptics wrong who told us when we moved here that "no one can farm organically in the Snoqualmie Valley and make a living at it,"—all these things too have been joys to me. But they don't drown out the troubling voices I hear.

What is important to you about the role that your farm plays in your community?

What is important to me is that our farm has been able to provide a point of reconnection to the earth for so many people, in so many ways. Some days as I conduct our "farm school" for the kids of our CSA members, I look at the faces of those 3–8 year old children and I feel so many things. I feel a responsibility to keep on trying, to keep on choosing the right path as a farmer rather than the easy path.

I also feel hope; hope for the future, that gives me the energy and motivation to do what I need to do today. It's really about doing.

Erick and Wendy Haakenson own and manage Jubilee Biodynamic Farm in Carnation, WA. Jubilee Farm endorses a commitment to the ontological conviction that people, animals, and every member of earth's biotic and non-biotic community are more than simply machines, that each has moral standing, and that therefore each is worthy of respect.

2012 will be Jubilee's 17th year of providing weekly boxes of produce to its CSA members. Erick also writes for his blog, The Growing Revolution:
www.jubileefarm.posterous.com
www.jubileefarm.org/thegrowingrevolution

Farmer Profile
Sean Conroe, Alleycat Acres Urban Farming Collective, Seattle, WA

Sean Conroe, founder of Alleycat Acres, is a social entrepreneur who has extensive experience with innovation and community capacity building.

Alleycat has this to say about their mission: "By farming the cityscape, we are helping to create solutions that address a number of issues facing our communities. Our urban farms lay the groundwork to enable anyone to join in the process of what we refer to as Farming 2.0: cultivating food, relationships, and a connection to our land in an urban setting."

How would you describe Alleycat Acres and its goals?

Alleycat Acres is a grassroots community farming project that works to build farms on otherwise empty urban space. We draw on the knowledge and wisdom from members of the communities where we are located to help us accomplish not only constructing these farms, but also the day-to-day growing processes.

To everyone involved, food is the cornerstone that creates the foundation for a healthy future. It is perhaps one of the most vital commonalities we all share—we all have to eat. It is through food that we believe we can learn more about each other, the city we live in and how we're all connected here—and elsewhere around the globe. Urban food systems touch on issues of social justice, transportation, health/nutrition and many others.

We see our farms as being spaces where we work toward a common goal of growing food and figuring out ways in which we can help solve some of these vital issues our generation is facing. It is a goal of ours to create these spaces to grow food and bridge communities. It's our goal to bring back agriculture into our cities. Our biggest goal, perhaps, is how to do all of this—sustainably.

What is the story of your involvement with this project? How did you get started?

The idea for Alleycat Acres arose during coursework at Seattle Central. I had been taking numerous classes, focusing on sustainable agriculture and communications. The idea was launched during the winter '09 quarter, where I built out a website that posed a simple question:
"Who wants to help create community run farms on vacant spaces in Seattle?"

From there, the response was amazing. I met with folks for about 3 weeks in late December - early January. All said and done, there were 11 original "Alleycats" each with a special area of knowledge. By the end of January, we had land offered to this project in Beacon Hill and by February 2010, we broke ground with more than 30 people who joined us.

Personally, this work is my passion. I grew up in rural western NY and was always out in the gardens and on farms and vineyards. It's always been a part of who I was—up until I moved to the city. For over 10 years, I had forgotten how powerful food + farming could be. Now, having been working on this for a year and a half, I'm reminded daily by seeing new faces and hands show up to work. I'm reminded by the kids from the neighborhoods who walk by and get excited about carrots and peas. Most of all, the stories that I learn about people and what food means to each of them cultivates this sense of connectedness and purpose—and it's what fuels me to keep going.

What are the main challenges that Alleycat Acres faces?

First and foremost, we learn by doing—a challenge in of itself. We're creating a model as we go along, looking to and working with other organizations for ideas on how to function. So far, it's resulted in more than 400 people on the farms, more than 1,000 pounds of food being grown and a network of more than 1,500 people who support us.

Time and funding are big challenges. There are five of us who are the main point people, working day and night behind the scenes. We do this as volunteers—balancing it with work, school and other commitments. To find funding to get people paid to do this takes time—something we all have very little of. It's a risk writing grant proposals—you never know if you'll get it. So far, we've spent our energy on fundraising, as we know something would result from it—what we've raised is more than enough to keep the farms growing and get what is needed.

How might the community support you in addressing these challenges?

We have an amazing core base of volunteers who keep the farms running for us. We're now starting to work more closely with people interested in other aspects of the organization: from communications and funding to outreach and bikes. Learning by doing takes time to accomplish some things, and we're slowly starting to figure out ways to solve some of the challenges.

What accomplishments are you most proud of?

There are many. However, what I'm most proud of is this letter we received from 3 students in 4th grade at Island Park Elementary School in Mercer Island, a school we've worked with throughout the year:

> *"Dear Alleycat Acres:*
> *We think how you garden is very interesting. Today we planted lots of seeds in cartons and watered them. We planted broccoli and peas and we hope they grow. You inspired us with the gardening."*

What makes me the most proud is that these kids are our future and they are able to experience food—a memory that will be with them for a lifetime.

What is important about the role that Alleycat Acres plays in your community?

Our work is not just "our" work; it's the result of the countless number of people who have ever stepped foot onto the farm or have helped in any area of the organization. For this reason, it serves an important role within our community: collectively we have a voice. And having a voice is but one of the many things needed to help grow forth.

*Sean Conroe's experimental approaches to social change activates marginalized populations who oftentimes lack a voice in social movements. His work with Alleycat Acres has been formally recognized by the American Institute of Architects, Sustainable Seattle and King County. Find the farm at **www.alleycatacres.com***

Global Stories of Change
Emerging Transnational Solutions

Farmers at the Table: Connecting Food and Trade Justice

Kristen Beifus, Washington Fair Trade Coalition
Colette Cosner, Witness for Peace Northwest
Claudia Navas, Community Alliance for Global Justice

When "Free Trade" Wins, Farmers, Land, & Communities Lose

Farmers are often named as the beneficiaries of U.S. Free Trade Agreements. It is reasoned that eliminating tariffs on agricultural goods imported to and exported from the U.S. and the trading partners established by these agreements levels the playing field. This allows farmers to sell more of the commodities they produce, increase jobs, and bring more prosperity into their communities.

This idea works if farmers are producing sufficient crops for themselves, local communities, and the global market. It assumes farmers and communities have appropriate infrastructure, such as roads and transport, as well as human and financial resources to access foreign markets. A "level playing field" also implies that farmers in different regions have comparable production means and costs, will produce and sell their particular commodities to countries that lack these crops, and that the global exchange for these crops will be fairly regulated so farmers get back more than they invest in the process.

If farmers were at the table crafting trade policy these conditions might exist and their communities would share more equally in trade prosperity. However, as trade agreements are being negotiated, it is large scale agribusiness lobbyists, business leaders, and politicians who are speaking for all farmers. Therefore the benefit is skewed in favor of these powerful corporate and political interests. U.S.

trade deals create incentives for agribusiness to move production out of the U.S. to countries where they can produce food as cheaply as possible and import it back into the U.S. with no tariffs. This drives down the price of food for consumers, but the costs are still in the global food supply chain, shouldered by farmers.

The costs are to farming communities throughout Latin America and the world whose people labor in industrial farms that grow food for the global north and receive poverty wages without rights as workers. The costs are to communities that are losing control of their natural resources—such as water and land and air—that are being privatized and polluted by foreign-owned factory farms.

The costs are the loss of farmers' knowledge of the land, appropriate technology, and sustainable growing as their lands are consolidated and planted with foreign seeds, that create high yielding crops protected with chemical pesticides and herbicides. The costs are to rural areas and cities as farmers are forced off their land to become workers on cash-crop farms while there is not enough food grown for their communities, or migrate to cities or other countries where they lack appropriate skills to find alternative work and so add to the growing communities living in poverty.

Free trade agreements are working for some as profits from international agribusiness continue to increase and shareholders enjoy higher yields on their investments. Companies also form alliances which augment gains and create an industry that further alienates the voices of farmers. When seed producers, chemical makers, and food companies team up, food production becomes more about what happens in boardrooms and laboratories than what is sown in fields.

Starting with the Andean Trade Preference Agreement in 1991, then the North American Free Trade Agreement (NAFTA) in 1994, the Central American Free Trade Agreement (CAFTA) in 2005, and the Peru Trade Promotion Agreement in 2009, U.S. has exported its model of trade to agricultural communities

To read about positive changes in fair trade advocacy in the United States, see Erin Thompson's article, "Domestic Fair Trade Association Makes Strides" on p. 50

throughout Latin America. More recently, in October of 2011, Congress passed three Free Trade Agreements , with Colombia, Panama, and South Korea, despite overwhelming opposition by various labor, environmental, and human rights groups in the U.S. and abroad.

Now in 2012, all eyes are focused on the Trans Pacific Partnership aka the Trans Pacific Free Trade Agreement (TP-FTA). Originally signed in June 2005 by the countries of Brunei Darussalam, Chile, New Zealand and Singapore, it was expanded in 2010 to include Peru, Australia, Vietnam, Malaysia and the US for a total of nine countries. The agreement has a 'docking clause' which means other Pacific Rim countries are able to join, and already Canada, Japan and Mexico have expressed interest in joining. This free trade agreement is momentous because of its expansive economic reach into many countries, as well as its political weight as President Obama's signature trade policy.

> The costs are to communities that are losing control of their natural resources; the costs are to rural areas and cities as farmers are forced off their land.

While the TP-FTA has been touted as promoting mutual economic growth among its members, it has been highly criticized by labor and global public health organizations. From what is known about this agreement it follows in the steps of past free trade agreements, that put Intellectual Property Rights ahead of communities' access to life-saving medicines and enables global corporations wider access to re-locate to countries where worker organizing is suppressed, and governments turn a blind-eye to workplace human rights abuses.

Even small-scale farmers who rely on local markets must frequently compete with cheaper food that is made in other countries, often by U.S. farming businesses already subsidized by our government with our tax dollars.

From Trade Justice to Food Justice: Organizing for Fair Trade Policy in Washington State

Injustices such as those mentioned above were what motivated Seattle-area activists to help organize the historic shutdown of the World Trade Organization meeting in 1999. From that, the Community Alliance for Global Justice sprouted and the energy continued into mobilizing against corporate-driven economic models and standing in solidarity with powerful social movements of the Global

South. In 2004, CAGJ joined with others across the hemisphere in resistance to the FTAA, an extension of NAFTA. After protests throughout the Americas, including an incredible week of action in Miami, the Free Trade Area of the Americas was defeated. The momentum continued with the near-defeat of CAFTA. In Washington State, CAGJ was successful in building the coalition that got all of Washington's Democratic Representatives in Congress to vote against the deal—a first!

From this success, CAGJ along with other labor, social justice and faith groups formed the Washington Fair Trade Coalition (WFTC). The WFTC now has 60 organizational members across WA State, working together to make US and WA state trade policy benefit farmers, workers and communities across the state, the nation and the globe.

> When seed producers, chemical makers, and food companies team up, food production becomes more about what happens in boardrooms and laboratories than what is sown in fields.

The inextricable link between corporate-led trade and investment policies and the failed industrial agricultural model is evident. Out of the seed of trade justice came the critical food justice and food sovereignty branch of Community Alliance for Global Justice. By supporting movements for healthy local food economies, in 2006, the focus shifted to building positive alternatives to corporate globalization. This shift was stamped with the first annual Strengthening Local Economies, Everywhere! Dinner. CAGJ stands with social movements around the world calling for Food Sovereignty, and supports our local farmers & other food producers who strengthen our local economy.

U.S. Agriculture vs. the Rest of the World

In developing its own agricultural system, the U.S. has historically protected our farmers by using high tariffs and investment to encourage U.S. citizens to support local farmers and hold back an invasion of cheap foreign goods. The U.S. Agricultural Industry remains one of the most protected in the world with tax incentives, subsidies, and tariffs. We need to provide the same protections for small-scale farmers in the U.S. and throughout the world.

We need to support vulnerable agricultural communities around the world, many recovering and reconstructing after decades of war, to develop appropriate agriculture, use local knowledge and resources, and access sustainable markets. This has led to agricultural prosperity in the U.S. and Europe.

We need to remember our history, of both long-term agricultural development and the more recent trade agreements that have dismantled it alongside the historic farming communities where we do business. And we need to have farmers at the table when developing trade policy. They are already at our tables each and every time we eat.

Farmers in the Field: The Faces of Trade Injustice

Baldemar Mendoza Jiménez
Union of Organizations of the Sierra Juarez of Oaxaca (UNOSJO)
Oaxaca, Mexico
NAFTA, implemented in 1994—More than 2 million Mexican Farmers Displaced (Institute for Agriculture and Trade Policy)

Mr. Mendoza works with indigenous communities to practice organic and traditional agriculture. He has participated in UNOSJO's informational campaign regarding the contamination of native corn by genetically modified corn. Mr. Mendoza promotes sustainable agriculture by using a "farmer-to-farmer" method to attain food sovereignty.

"NAFTA took away price guarantees for corn and other products," says Mendoza. "Farmers could not make ends meet and looked for alternatives that would generate income. They abandoned their lands, they left to work in maquilas, and they emigrated to the United States. Migration has brought the abandonment of the countryside, family disintegration, and a decomposition of the tightly-woven community. Community practices that were an integral part to indigenous Oaxacan communities have been lost."

From the 2009 Witness for Peace Northwest speaking tour, "The Legacy of NAFTA"

Augusto Obregon

Community Leader and Small-Scale Farmer, Estelí, Nicaragua

Dominican Republic Central American-United States Free Trade Agreement (CAFTA-DR), implemented in 2005—Hundreds of thousands of Central American Farmers Displaced

"Free trade agreements, neo-liberal policies, and aid conditions from international financial institutions have brought Nicaragua to extreme poverty. Desperate to work for their families, people migrate to countries such as Costa Rica, Spain, and the U.S. In my community, El Regardio, a tobacco factory was installed under the free trade zone. Although it generated employment, the salaries are miserable. It also contaminates the environment, principally the water supply, and causes diseases, mainly with women and children. Some farmers are selling their land to cultivate tobacco, causing less production of food. This continues not only to harm the health of the community, but also fails to feed them"

From the 2010 Witness for Peace Northwest speaking tour, "The Roots of Migration"

Uriel Tuberquin

Displaced Family Farmer, Colombia

Displaced People due to decades long conflict: 4 million

Colombia-U.S. Free Trade Agreement—Predicted Colombian farmers further displaced: Tens of thousands

"When we were displaced, our land was robbed from us and filled with monoculture crops like palm oil and bananas. These mega-projects forcibly displaced us from our lands, placing us, the small-scale farmers, in the middle of a very violent conflict. We want to live in peace, we want our land returned to us, and we want justice."

From the 2010 "Face the Displaced" action toolkit, created by Witness for Peace Northwest

Washington State's Asparagus Farmers

Andean Trade Preference Act, which became the Peru-U.S. TPA 1991/2006—three fifths of asparagus acreage lost in Washington State

U.S. Trade Policy with the Andean countries highlights the case of asparagus. As a substitution crop for coca, the U.S. subsidized the growth of an asparagus industry. Policies introduced a cash crop that was little grown in the region, and the reduction in import tariffs into the U.S. encouraged big asparagus companies such as Green Giant and Del Monte to leave Washington State to set up large-scale farms throughout the Andes. Farmers in Washington lost more than half of their asparagus industry and farmers in the Andes, notably Peru, were hired as workers on industrial farm complexes.

Kristen Beifus lives in Seattle, where she enjoys walking amongst the trees, improv dancing, and working to change global trade policy with the Washington Fair Trade Coalition.

Colette Cosner was the Regional Organizer of Witness for Peace Northwest from 2009-2011. She is also a board member of the Washington Fair Trade Coalition.

Claudia Navas is traveling around the east coast where she is sight-seeing, spending time with family, visiting friends and checking out local farms & markets.

Bibliography:

Allen, Patricia. 2008 *Mining for Justice in the Food System: Perceptions, Practices, and Possibilities*. Agriculture and Human Values 25: 157-161.

Allen, Patricia and Alice Brooke Wilson. 2008 *Agrifood Inequalities: Globalization and Localization*. Development 51(4):534-540.

Schiavoni, Christina. 2009 *The Global Struggle for Food Sovereignty: From Nyéléni to New York*. The Journal of Peasant Studies. 36(3):682-689.ti

Resources: www.washingtonfairtrade.org
www.citizenstrade.org

Mutirão in the Favelas: Confronting the Global Food Crisis one Community at a Time

Rob Sawers

SÃO PAULO, BRAZIL—Brazil is currently undergoing profound economic changes. Prices are soaring, investment is growing, and the number of Brazilian billionaires is multiplying. In São Paulo, a sprawling metropolis of twenty million people, the rich travel through the city by helicopter, and the poor are being told that Brazil will rank as a developed nation by the year 2016.[1] As the country looks forward to hosting the FIFA World Cup and the Summer Olympics in the coming years, Brazil hopes it can now pose as a nation safe for foreign investment and tourism.

But while the global economic downturn is nowhere to be seen in this up-and-coming "investment paradise,"[2] the global food crisis is in full swing. The world's largest agricultural economy after China, Brazil is at the epicenter of this crisis, and is not immune to its catastrophic effects. As ever greater swathes of the Amazon basin are burnt and bulldozed to make way for soy plantations, cattle ranches, and hydroelectric dams,[3] Brazil's agricultural interior will become more prone to environmental disasters, degradation of soil fertility, desertification,

---

1   Osava, Maria. "WSF: Reconciling Social and Environmental Needs." *Terra Viva: World Social Forum 2011.* *www.ips.org/TV/wsf/wsf-reconciling-social-and-environmental-needs/*

2   Heller, Reginaldo, translated by Rosemary Baptista. "Brazil: An Investment Paradise in a World in Crisis." *Discover Brazil Magazine.* July (2010). p. 10

3   Barona, Elizabeth. "The Role of Pasture and Soybean in the Deforestation of the Brazilian Amazon." *Environmental Research Letters.* V.5 (2010). p.1-2

and species extinction.[4] The environmental carnage alone is cause for alarm and outrage, but this process is also a social one, as farmers, indigenous groups, and all sorts of rural peoples are forced to sell or abandon their land, and move to the slums that ring every city in this country. Environmental degradation is not solely an attack on natural beauty, but also an attack on human dignity and will result in unprecedented human misery in a country already suffering some of the world's highest rates of inequality.[5]

In Brazilian Portuguese, the word *mutirão* is roughly translated as communal work, or people coming together to work for social betterment.

These transformations in Brazil's agrarian interior can already be observed from the check-out register of any supermarket in the country. In this land of agricultural bounty and luxurious tropical fruits and vegetables, prices for general food stuffs have steadily increased[6] to the point where the poor are forced to survive on a diet of little more than fried dough, rice, and beans. In the slums (*favelas* in Portuguese), people simply cannot keep up with the price hikes in supermarkets, and they are worried for their immediate future.

Shoots of Resistance

Clearly, solutions are needed, and many have lost their patience with the empty promises of politicians and have decided to take charge of their own futures. If food prices have become so wildly manipulated by commodities brokers and international supermarket chains that the poor cannot afford vegetables, then they will simply grow their own. Across Brazil, people in the *favelas* have started clearing the trash from unused and wasted space and planting vegetables for their own communities. These are 'do-it-yourself' projects for and by entire communities that refuse to be abused by the corporations and politicians that are deaf to the calls for agrarian reform and social welfare.

4   Kinver, Mark. "Amazon Forest Fires 'On the Rise.'" *BBC World News Online.* June, 6, 2010. www. bbc.co.uk/news/10228989.

5   GINI coefficient of 54 in 2009. "World Development Indicators, 2011" World Bank. data.worldbank.org /indicator/SI.POV.GINI,.

6   Lora, E., Andrew Powell, and Pilar Tavella. "How will the Food Price Shock Affect Inflation in Latin America and the Caribbean?" *Inter-American Development Bank, Policy Brief.* N.120. (April, 2011). 2.

One urban gardening group, Cities Without Hunger (*Organização Cidades Sem Fome*), operates over twenty organic gardens spread throughout São Paulo's *favelas*, provides employment for hundreds of people, mostly women and certain at-risk groups,[7] and grows vegetables for thousands of poor and unemployed people. Having recently attracted international acclaim for its practices,[8] the movement is intensifying its search for unused patches of land in the city, and reaching out to more and more communities to reproduce their successful model. Incredibly, Cities Without Hunger acts like an organic farming cooperative spread throughout one of the largest metropolises in the world.

The rewards of urban gardening are immediate and obvious to those who otherwise would have absolutely no access to fresh fruits and vegetables, not to mention organic or local produce. The founder of Cities Without Hunger, Hans Dieter Temp, encourages first-time gardeners to start with vegetables like lettuce and radishes. The idea is to start with plants that grow the fastest, so that the gardeners can see the monetary and dietary benefits as soon as possible. Later on, gardeners are encouraged take on a broader variety of vegetables for greater nutritional diversity. Gardeners who work with Cities Without Hunger are now cultivating a wide range of crops, including a variety of local vegetables like *chuchu*. The movement has even begun implementing plans for orchard and tree fruit production.

"Conformity to Misery"

Temp's work involves negotiating with landlords of unused land to allow gardens to take root, testing soil quality for toxins in potential sites, and gathering materials for the organization. But according to him, one of the most challenging aspects of his job is convincing those in the *favelas* that gardening is in fact worth their while. This includes breaking through the thick defensive mentality of fatalism that develops among the desperately poor. This "conformity to misery," as Temp's wife Rachel put it during a visit to the gardens, is an understandable attitude to take when one is surrounded by unemployment and drug abuse. Stand-

---

7   *This includes the elderly, disabled, recovering substance abusers, and the homeless.*

8   *Dubai International Award for Best Practices, 2011. Chowdhury, Farhana. "12 Projects Win Dubai Award for Best Practices" Khaleej Times Online. March 30, 2011. www.khaleejtimes.ae*

ing between rows of radish plants in the notoriously poor *Favela Sabopemba,* Temp recalled how difficult it was to convince the women of the neighborhood that they themselves were capable of making a difference to their community. When showed the lush garden already up and running in a neighboring *favela,* the women of *Sabopemba* were, at first, surprisingly un-moved. The sentiment the women seemed to be expressing was one of inferiority: *"How could we replicate something so beautiful?"*

The women of *Sabopemba* did eventually join Cities Without Hunger, and the act of collective gardening has begun to chip away at the mentality of failure. These women have given their children and neighbors something truly rare in the slums: pride and empowerment in their communities and in themselves. In Brazilian Portuguese, the word *mutirão* is roughly translated as communal work, or people coming together to work for social betterment. It is the spirit of *mutirão* that has brought many together to clear the trash from public spaces and begin tilling the soil in the midst of Brazil's concrete jungles. In this way, *mutirão* rejects the psychological as well as the practical disorders of poverty.

Daily Poverty

While urban hunger is a product of an over-arching inequality and poverty, aided and abetted by the crushing psychology of social apartheid, some obstacles to a family getting enough healthy food are not theoretical but frustratingly practical. Grocery stores, in addition to being too expensive for the average slum resident, are almost all located far from the *favelas* and inaccessible by public transportation. A mother with mouths to feed who does laundry for middle-class families on the other side this mega-metropolis, might have to take multiple buses (which cost money) to get to and from a supermarket. With this sort of epic commute, a head of lettuce or a few ripe mangos would be bruised and crushed by the time she gets home to cook dinner. While this sort of problem may seem utterly mundane and not relevant to the realities of poverty, many in the *Favela Sabopemba* have pointed to exactly these types of situations as obstacles to good nutrition. Faced with the prospect of arriving home with ruined lettuce that they could barely afford, most simply opt for the cheap and the reliable: rice, noodles, and *farofa.*[9] Repeatedly, Temp could not stress enough how the mundane and quotidian details shape the realities of urban poverty.

The Corporate Grip on Food Markets

What is needed, and what Cities Without Hunger hope to be a small part of, is a move away from large-scale, industrial agriculture and the supermarket chains that distribute its produce. In Brazil, and indeed in the United States as well, giant corporations control much of the country's agricultural production.[10] The corporate model for agriculture relies on massive government subsidies, crop specialization and intensification, and uses expensive machinery and chemicals. Against these Goliaths of production, smallholder and family farms have little chance to stay competitive. Small farms rack up debt and foreclose, and the grip of the corporate giants on agriculture strengthens, even at a time when the UN-FAO has begun openly admitting a Global Food Crisis.[11]

These vertically integrated agribusiness corporations, in turn, rely on supermarkets as the mechanism for raking in their profits. But as noted above, supermarkets in themselves can be the stage on which the drama of social exclusion is played. Supermarkets are the primary access to fresh foods for a rapidly growing percentage of the planet's population.[12] They present the consumer with a dazzling array of goods and the producer with branding and packaging that cultivates brand recognition and loyalty. But in these highly profitable corporate paradises, shoppers divide themselves along class lines based on what they can afford and what groceries will survive the long bus-ride home. Rich and poor alike may shop at the same stores, but leave with very different purchases.

> The women of *Sabopemba* did eventually join Cities Without Hunger, and the act of collective gardening has begun to chip away at the mentality of failure.

9   A common food in Brazil, *farofa* is nutrient-poor, toasted cassava flour that is mixed with black bean stew as a thickener.

10   Holt-Gimenez, Eric. "Onward Corporate Crusaders." *Huffington Post.* February 7, 2011. www.huffington post.com/eric-holt-gimenez/onward-corporate-food-cru_b_817058.html.

11   GRAIN.org "Getting Out of the Food Crisis." *Seedling.* July 2008. www.grain.org/seedling/?id=550.

12   Reardon, Thomas. et al. "Supermarkets in Africa, Asia, and Latin America." *American Journal of Agricultural Economics.* V.85. No.5 (2003) 1141.

The division is equally stark between classes of producers. Many small farmers simply cannot stay in business selling their produce to supermarkets because the supermarkets pay artificially low wholesale prices. For instance, the French supermarket chain Carrefour is very powerful in Brazil with 50 million consumers and nearly five hundred stores in and around São Paulo.[13] At the time that the interviews for this article were conducted, Carrefour in São Paulo was paying farmers 6 centavos (approximately 4 US cents) for a head of lettuce. For those with hundreds of thousands of hectares, and millions or billions to spend on advanced machinery and chemicals, it is possible to turn a profit on lettuce at six *centavos* a head. But for farmers on small plots trying to compete, it is simply not profitable to cultivate crops. They would be better off moving to the city to do someone else's laundry or sell drugs on the street; and so the pattern of rural decay continues. This is the unjust reality of production and consumption that many in Brazil are trying to resist.

> What is developing across Brazil are networks of small farmers, cooperatives, agronomists, and social movements that is being called the Solidarity Economy.

To confront both sides of this challenge to slum residents, Cities Without Hunger cultivates gardens large enough to be economically productive, and not simply a nutritional life-line. Producing at a surplus leads to the development of farmers' markets for local, organic fruits and vegetables in neighborhoods that have never before had such luxuries. The markets are, indeed, one of the most exciting aspects of Cities Without Hunger's model, because it begins to chip away at the nutritional apartheid that divides Brazil between rich and poor. In addition to the pride and self-worth that comes from neighbors working together in *mutirão* at these markets, the low prices give access to fresh produce for a much broader section of the population. A head of lettuce at these markets sells for 1 *Real* (approximately 60 cents); compared to Carrefour, this is a lower price for the consumer and much higher revenue for the producer.[14]

The fact that prices at these farmer's markets for fresh vegetables are lower than those at the supermarket[15] is partially due to the absence of middle-men. As

13   *Ibid.1144.*

14   *Interview with Hans Dieter Temp, founder of Organização Cidades Sem Fome (Cities Without Hunger), conducted by Rob Sawers in São Paulo, Brazil on November 23, 2010.*

15   *Minten, B. and Thomas Reardon. "Food Prices, Quality, and Quality's Pricing in Supermarkets versus Traditional Markets in Developing Countries" Review of Agricultural Economics. V.30. N.3. (2008) 488.*

noted above in the example about Carrefour's pricing structure for lettuce, corporate supermarkets require a huge discrepancy between wholesale and retail prices for fresh produce, to sustain the overhead costs of entire international corporations. Supermarket prices include the initial price of the goods, but also the costs of employing thousands in countless specialized industries such as shipping, food processing, and agribusiness research and development spread throughout the world. From the supermarket staff all the way up through engineers and mechanics, administrative offices, legal teams, financial advisors, executives, and board members, it is the farmers and consumers who are ultimately paying the bill. But why is it that struggling farmers and the destitute slum-dwellers are forced to take part in such an overbearing and unjust structure? Why are the women of *Favela Sabopemba* contributing to the benefits packages of Carrefour's board of trustees?

These world-famous groups are only the most visible in a chorus of smaller social movements that are transforming Brazil's agrarian economy and creating an alternative mindset for development.

The Solidarity Economy

As a development model or a solution to the global food crisis, some would claim that the vegetable gardening and farmers' markets model is small potatoes, and that it is simply a band-aid for a food production system that is spinning out of control. This may well be the case, and the long-term solutions lie not in the cities that consume, but in the country that produces. Peasants and smallholders across the world are clamoring for agrarian reform as the capital-intensive, food producing machine bruises more land and renders more local markets obsolete. But as the farmers' struggle marches on, out of sight and out of mind for the majority of Earth's urban population, the marginalized majority cannot continue waiting for the promised development to reach them. With food prices spiraling to ludicrous heights, looking forward to being served the fruits of someone else's capitalism is a fantasy they can no longer afford.

What is developing across Brazil are networks of small farmers, cooperatives, agronomists, and social movements that is being called the Solidarity Economy.[16] Groups like the Landless Workers' Movement (MST—*Movimento dos*

---

16   Eid, F. and Andréa Eloisa Buena Pimentel. "Solidarity Economy: Challenges of Cooperative Agrarian Reform in Brazil." *Journal of Rural Cooperation*. V.29. N.2. (2001). 1.

Trabalhadores Rurais Sem-Terra) and Via Campesina among others, are looking for ways to empower small farmers and encourage agricultural practices that are in-tune with the fragile ecosystems of the Amazon and its periphery. And these world-famous groups are only the most visible in a chorus of smaller social movements that are transforming Brazil's agrarian economy and creating an alternative mindset for Brazilian development. One of the main challenges to this movement, apart from securing land and political will, is finding a method of distributing produce that sidelines the supermarkets and all the problems they generate. That is why Cities Without Hunger's organic vegetable markets in the favelas are so important. Not only do the gardens and markets put organic produce directly in the hands of those who need it most desperately, but they play a small role in supporting this brave step away from a system that destroys economies, habitats, and families.

Rob Sawers lives in Teresina, Piauí, in northern Brazil where he enjoys teaching English and writing about social justice on the edge of the Amazon.

Works Cited:

Barona, Elizabeth. "The Role of Pasture and Soybean in the Deforestation of the Brazilian Amazon." Environmental Research Letters. V.5 (2010).

Chowdhury, Farhana. "12 Projects Win Dubai Award for Best Practices" Khaleej Times Online. March 30, 2011. www.khaleejtimes.ae

Eid, F. and Andréa Eloisa Buena Pimentel. "Solidarity Economy: Challenges of Cooperative Agrarian Reform in Brazil." Journal of Rural Cooperation. V.29. N.2. (2001).

GRAIN.org "Getting Out of the Food Crisis." Seedling. July 2008. www.grain.org

Heller, Reginaldo, translated by Rosemary Baptista. "Brazil: An Investment Paradise in a World in Crisis." Discover Brazil Magazine. July (2010).

Holt-Gimenez, Eirc. "Onward Corporate Crusaders." Huffington Post. February 7, 2011. www.huffingtonpost.com

Lora, E., Andrew Powell, and Pilar Tavella. "How will the Food Price Shock Affect Inflation in Latin America and the Caribbean?" Inter-American Development Bank, Policy Brief. N.120. (April, 2011).

Minten, B. and Thomas Reardon. "Food Prices, Quality, and Quality's Pricing in Supermarkets versus Traditional Markets in Developing Countries" Review of Agricultural Economics. V.30. N.3. (2008) p.480-490.

Kinver, Mark. "Amazon Forest Fires 'On the Rise.'" BBC World News Online. June, 6, 2010. www.bbc.co.uk/news/10228989.

Reardon, Thomas. et al. "Supermarkets in Africa, Asia, and Latin America." American Journal of Agricultural Economics. V.85. No.5 (2003) 1140-1146.

Osava, Maria. "WSF: Reconciling Social and Environmental Needs." Terra Viva: World Social Forum 2011. www.ips.org/TV/wsf/wsf-reconciling-social-and-environmental-needs/.

World Development Indicators, 2011.World Bank. data.worldbank.org/indicator/SI.POV.GINI

Feminine Fortitude in the World Food System: Women's Contributions to Food Sovereignty

Erica Bacon

Let us take a journey: a voyage through a reality in which the inter-dependence of all living beings is acknowledged; a reality in which the health and well being of all creatures, cultures and living systems is recognized for its intrinsic value; a reality in which we as humans relate to one another and to the natural world in a way that exhibits the utmost degree of compassion and understanding, a relational style free of oppression, hierarchy and dogmatic tendencies.

A world like this one is articulated through the principles of *ecofeminism*, described by Vandana Shiva as "the democracy of all life." Patriarchy, the global epidemic of a social system that feeds on the domination of women and nature, has created a reality counter to the one above. The injustices within the world food system provide a very clear lens through which we can view gender inequality as well as other systems of oppression such as racism and classism—and, I believe, also serve to highlight a very clear starting point at which we can affect change. It is entirely possible for the former world to exist; the fundamental shift in consciousness required to fuel such a transition will begin with a reconnection to the feminine and through a more comprehensive understanding of the world food system and its deeply entrenched gender inequalities.

The decomposition of patriarchal systems that dominate women and the natural world and marginalize people and cultures of less privilege is beginning; this process will provide the compost that we need to create the revolution that we want to see.

Around the world, women are working to shift the direction of the globalized industrial food system by reconnecting with their roots. From women in Bellingham, Washington mobilizing to advocate for food justice and immigrants rights; to mothers in Detroit's "food deserts"[1] growing their own food so that their children have access to fresh produce; to women-led seed saving projects in Africa, India and elsewhere in the Global South resisting corporate control of the seed market; fresh patches of eco-feminism are germinating and re-defining the way that we eat and interact with food, community and the environment.

It is no secret that women, particularly women of color, are disproportionately affected by the injustices within the world food system.

The reality is, the journey we are embarking on is a complicated one and must be understood in the context of patriarchy, colonialism and all subsequent forms of hierarchy and oppression. Each inspirational story of progress is surrounded with unsettling truths and statistics that help to illustrate why this shift that we are beginning to see is necessary and can help us all to realize that we must work together and ensure that the "compost" is well tended to so that progress can continue.

It is no secret that women, particularly women of color, are disproportionately affected by the injustices within the world food system. Women make up the majority of the world's food producers, but they are also the most likely to be *food insecure*. Among developing countries, rural women retain the majority of the responsibility for domestic food production through labor, processing and cooking. They play a major role in the trade of fresh produce and processed food products and play an essential role in seed saving projects that allow the world's poor to continue farming (Jiggens).

1   *The language in the 2008 Farm Bill defi ned a food desert as an "area in the United States with limited access to affordable and nutritious food, particularly such an area composed of predominantly lower income neighborhoods and communities" (Title VI, Sec. 7527).*

"Import reliance"—caused by colonialism and colonial trade patterns, Free Trade Agreements (for the United States) and Economic Partnership Agreements (for the European Union), structural adjustment policies promoted by the World Bank and the International Monetary Fund and US food aid policy, among other things—creates a reality where it becomes far less expensive for consumers in the Global South to purchase imported foods than it is for consumers to buy from farmers within their own communities. As this continues, women relying on agriculture for income are having more trouble making ends meet.

Transnational corporations and foreign governments are buying and leasing farmland in the most fertile and productive regions of the Global South to grow food that will be exported far from the communities in which it is grown. This land-grabbing results in more and more small-scale farmers being driven into urban areas. Those farmers who do find work on industrial scale farms are often grossly underpaid, abused and exploited; many of them are women. Multinational corporations, like Dupont and Monsanto, now have patents on seed types that have been saved and cultivated by generations of women farmers, making it illegal for small farmers to save those seeds, and selling them at a high price. In addition, the rural-urban migration of men puts higher labor demands on women who are often left behind to work the land.

> Fresh patches of eco-feminism are germinating and re-defining the way that we eat and interact with food, community and the environment.

In direct resistance and opposition to the globalization of food and seed markets, women continue saving seed in an attempt to preserve both cultural integrity and biological and crop diversity. In India, the women-centered network of seed keepers and organic producers spanning across 16 states, *Navdanya* (meaning both "nine seeds" and "new gift") works to save and distribute seed throughout the country. They have worked to set up 54 community seed banks and aided in the organization of the largest direct marketing, fair trade organic network in the country.

Through Navdanya, over half a million farmers have been trained in seed sovereignty, food sovereignty, and sustainable agriculture. They run a learning center in Northern India on an organic farm called *Bija Vidyapeeth*—meaning "the School of the Seed"—and are working to raise awareness about the danger of genetic engineering, and serving to inform people about their food rights and about the threat of *biopiracy* (the appropriation and privatization of indigenous genetic wealth and knowledge) in the face of globalization and climate change. (www.navdanya.org)

In Africa, women are organizing across the continent to confront the Gates and Rockefeller Foundation-funded "Green Revolution" which pushes GMOS while creating dependence on high yield seeds, as well as costly chemical pesticides and fertilizers. In many parts of the world the Green Revolution has driven small-holder farmers off the land and into greater poverty.

One campaign led by African women farmers is called "We are the Solution: Celebrating Family Farming in Africa." It involves rural women's associations, community leaders, and farmer federations in an effort to improve, promote, and share traditional agricultural knowledge and practices as a viable alternative to Green Revolution methods. The women's campaign was officially launched during the World Social Forum in Dakar, Senegal in February 2011 with the following objectives: (newfieldfound.org)

This is food sovereignty in action. For a definition and discussion of food sovereignty, see La Via Campesina's "Seven Principles of Food Sovereignty" on p. 18

· *To strengthen the work of 12 rural women's associations and their leaders through organizational and individual capacity building activities;*

· *To facilitate the participation of 75 rural women participants in media and advocacy activities so that they can engage in decision-making processes in local, regional and global campaigns;*

· *To mobilize and sustain an Africa-wide action-oriented network of 1,000 stake-holders for information sharing, partnership and advocacy.*

Meanwhile, in the United States and other "developed" nations, women play a role at least equally significant in food production, processing and preparation. As a result of structural racism and sexism, the disproportionate burden of injustices carried by women within the food system is sobering. Gender inequality in the world food system is linked to poverty, hunger and poor health (Pan, Wen-Harn et al).

According to data collected by the USDA in 2009, households with the highest rates of food insecurity included those with children; households with children headed by single women make up 36.6 percent of those who are food insecure. Nearly 25 percent of households experiencing food insecurity were Black non-Hispanic households and about 27 percent were Hispanic households (Feeding America).

Mothers and children face a particularly high risk of malnutrition and poor-diet related illness due to the fact that pregnant and nursing mothers have elevated nutritional needs and are not afforded the same access to fulfill those needs in a sexist and classist system.

In Detroit, concerned mothers from the Nsoroma Institute banded together after the last of the city's major grocery stores left in 2006, leaving residents (largely African American) with only corner stores and mini-marts at which to purchase food. Concerned for their childrens' health and nutrition, they decided to take matters into their own hands and begin growing their own food as a community.

In India, over half a million farmers have been trained in seed sovereignty, food sovereignty, and sustainable agriculture.

Their project has evolved enormously over the past several years and has become what is now D-town Farm, a two acre farm in Northwestern Detroit's Rouge Park. Although leadership of D-town, and the Detroit Black Community Food Security Network (DBCFSN) through which the farm is run, is multi-gendered, women continue to play a formative role in increasing the community's food sovereignty. In addition to farming and sustainable agriculture education, the DBCFSN works on food policy issues, and runs Ujamaa Food Co-op Buying Club, which offers organic and healthy food choices to members who would otherwise not have access to such foods. (detroitblackfoodsecurity.org)

Female food workers are subject to employment discrimination, wage discrimination, sexual harassment, sexual assault and other forms of sexual exploitation. According to the Applied Research Center's The Color of Food, for every dollar in median wage earned by a white man, an Asian woman will earn 68 cents, a white woman 63 cents, a black woman 53 cents and a Latina woman will earn 50 cents.

Women represent an estimated 630,000 farm workers in the United States (National Agricultural Workers Survey). Of farm worker women interviewed in California by Maria Elena Trevino of the Southern Poverty Law Center (SPLC), 90 percent reported sexual harassment as a major problem; among low wage immigrant women interviewed in the Southeastern United States by the SPLC, 77 percent reported that sexual violence was a major problem.

The Equal Employment Opportunities Commission learned through an investigation of farmworker women that in California, one company's fields are known as *"field de calzon"* (fields of panties) because so many women are raped and sexually assaulted by their supervisors. In Florida, female farm workers call the fields "green motels" for the same reason. In Iowa, women attested that they had encountered sexual abuse so often that they believed it to be common practice in the United States to exchange sex for job security (Southern Poverty Law Center: Injustice on Our Plates).

> In Africa, women are organizing across the continent to confront the Green Revolution's dependence on high-yield seeds and costly chemical pesticides and fertilizers.

Recognizing the extraordinary injustices that women face (especially undocumented immigrant women), organizations such as Bellingham's Community to Community Development (C2C) are mobilizing to promote food justice, movement building and participatory democracy. Based on ideals of egalitarianism, C2C is a women-of-color led organization and calls attention to the fact that women, people of color and poor and low income communities are denied equal access to justice and rights that protect human dignity under US law. Their social justice work is self described as being

> "...focused on creating movement towards the creation of communities that: empower under-represented peoples to have an equal voice in decision making processes that affect their lives; develop and strengthen cross cultural awareness; restore justice to our food, land and cultural practices, promote community relationships towards self reliance and stand in solidarity with organizations working for human and civil rights."

Program areas are brought to action through participatory, community based and led projects that are knit together through ecofeminist and food justice lenses. (www.foodjustice.org)

The journey towards Vandana Shiva's vision of "a democracy of all life" will be long, it will be turbulent, and it will be tumultuous. If we pay close attention to the scenery, though, we will notice the pockets of strength, beauty and wonder that already exist and that are being newly cultivated by women and their allies. They possess the knowledge that working with genuine care and concern for one another and for the Earth is the only way to create a healthy food system and a healthy world.

By strengthening the food sovereignty within our own communities, and by raising awareness about our discontent with the continued globalization of the patriarchial, racist and classist ideologies and technologies that are undermining our collective health, we can create an alternative reality. We already are.

Erica Bacon lives at an Urban Farming Cooperative in Seattle, Washington where she helps to grow food, raise chickens and cultivate community. She volunteers with CAGJ's Food Justice Project.

References:

Agarwal, Bina. Food Crisis and Gender Inequality. DESA Working Paper no. 107. June 2011. www.un.org/esa/desa/papers/2011/wp107_2011.pdf

Community to Community Development. www.foodjustice.org

Detroit Black Community Food Security Network. www.detroitblackfoodsecurity.org

Feeding America. 2011. www.feedingamerica.org/hunger-in-america/hunger-facts/hunger-and-poverty-statistics.aspx

International Museum of Women: Women, Power and Politics. Seeds of Resistance. 2008. www.imow.org/wpp/stories/viewStory?storyId=1236

Jiggens, Janice. Foresight Project on Global Food and Farming Futures. Gender in the Food System. www.bis.gov.uk/assets/.../food.../11-585-sr48-gender-in-the-food-system

National Agricultural Workers Survey. www.doleta.gov/agworker/naws.cfm

Navdanya. www.navdanya.org

Pan, Wen-Harn et all. Gender Specific Roles and Needs in Food and Health Security. 2009. www.ncbi.nlm.nih.gov/pubmed/19965359

Ramirez, Monica. *25 Years After Landmark Meritor Decision, Immigrant Women Still Face Workplace Sexual Violence.* June 2011. http://www.splcenter.org/get-informed/news/25-years-after-landmark-meritor-decision-immigrant-women-still-face-workplace-sexual-violence

Southern Poverty Law Center. Injustice on Our Plates. www.splcenter.org/get-informed/publications/injustice-on-our-plates

Women Watch. Gender Equality and Trade Policy. 2011. www.un.org/womenwatch/feature/trade/

Resistance is Fertile: Grassroots Alternatives to a Green Revolution for Africa

Janae Choquette, AGRA Watch Co-Chair

The tides are beginning to turn. Over the past few years, wave after wave of new reports has joined the growing swell of scientific literature confirming what people in the food movement have been saying for a long time: small-scale, agroecological farming is the future. Contrary to the dominant corporate narrative that we need industrial agriculture and genetically modified (GM) crops to feed the world, reports such as the UN and World Bank-funded International Assessment of Agricultural Knowledge, Science, and Technology for Development (IAASTD) paint a very different picture—and ultimately conclude that the challenges of the 21st century require moving away from agri-"business as usual".

Over 400 scientists from 80 countries participated in the 2008 IAASTD, the most comprehensive survey of global agricultural practices, policies, and institutions ever undertaken. Its findings were so unfavorable to industry that agribusiness giant Monsanto, involved in the initial phases, pulled out of the project entirely, as did the World Bank.

What was it that Monsanto didn't want the world to know? For starters, that the high productivity of industrial agriculture has come with even higher costs— degraded soil and water, loss of biodiversity, greenhouse gas emissions, severe health problems, increased social inequity—and with gains exclusive to a wealthy few. Even more damning, the IAASTD warned that high tech fixes like GM crops are, at best, unlikely to make a dent in world hunger and, at worst, likely to exacerbate the social and environmental problems behind it.

So what's the alternative? According to a 2010 report by Olivier de Schutter, UN Special Rapporteur on the Right to Food, "eco-farming" projects throughout the Global South have demonstrated the potential to more than double production in food insecure areas while mitigating climate change. Examples of eco-farming systems in the report are each unique, but they share common principles based in *agroecology*, the science behind sustainable agriculture.

> "Eco-farming" projects throughout the Global South have demonstrated the potential to more than double production in food insecure areas while mitigating climate change.

Agroecology sees the farm as an ecosystem, and applies ecological principles to farming accordingly. In designing agricultural systems, agroecology draws on natural processes to minimize resource use, preserve the environment, and maximize production—all without expensive, corporate-controlled inputs.

This kind of farming is knowledge-intensive rather than high-tech—as each system is adapted to the conditions of its local environment—and empowers farmers as researchers and innovators in their own fields. It also reduces their dependency on transnational corporations and volatile global markets, since farmers save their own seeds, produce their own fertilizers, and grow most of their crops for local consumption.

Farmers, scientists, and development experts around the world are echoing the findings of these reports, insisting that agroecological farming is our best chance to end hunger and cool the planet. A radical transformation of the way we produce, distribute, and eat food is necessary, and given the magnitude of the economic and environmental crises we currently face, we had better get moving.

Yet governments, policymakers, and philanthropic organizations have been slow to turn the boat around, unwilling or unable to respond to this powerful call for a new direction. They continue to promote industrial agriculture and the adoption of GM crops as solutions to hunger and climate change.

One striking example of this wrong-headed approach and the very real threat it poses to viable alternatives is the push for a second Green Revolution in Africa led by the Bill and Melinda Gates Foundation.

Based on the premise that Africa is starving because it "missed" the first Green Revolution, the Gates Foundation has poured millions of dollars into bringing the "miracle technologies" of the Green Revolution—chemical fertilizers, herbicides and pesticides, high-yielding seed varieties—to the continent through its Alliance for a Green Revolution in Africa (AGRA) initiative.

Often hailed as having saved the world from mass famine, the original Green Revolution focused on achieving higher yields through mechanization and monoculture of "improved" hybrid crops. It introduced a one-size-fits-all approach to farming that imitates industry (unlike agroecology, which imitates nature) and requires heavy inputs of water, agro-chemicals, and fossil fuels.

In its narrowly-defined crusade to boost productivity, the original Green Revolution was extremely successful, a triumph of modern agricultural technology. But by other social and ecological measures, the results weren't nearly as glowing.

Though worldwide food production per capita increased by 11 percent, hunger kept pace and grew between 11-19% during the same period, particularly in regions where the Green Revolution had taken root (ie. parts of Latin America and Southeast Asia). In other words, food production and food insecurity increased side by side.

This paradox makes sense when we take a closer look at what was happening on the ground, particularly throughout the Global South. The Green Revolution model required expensive inputs and a scaling-up of agriculture that, in the end, benefitted only a handful of wealthy farmers. Millions of small-scale farmers (a majority of them women) and indigenous peoples were driven into debt, pushed off their lands, and shunted into urban slums without employment opportunities. This model also geared production toward global markets rather than local consumption, constricting local food supply at the same time that more and more people could no longer grow their own food or afford to buy it.

Thika, Nairobi, and Kitale, Kenya: 2010 visit by CAGJ members

In 2010 CAGJ's Director, Heather Day, and her husband Travis English traveled to Kenya to research the Gates Foundation's *Alliance for a Green Revolution in Africa (AGRA)*, and to visit grassroots efforts to promote alternatives. They spent time with members of *Kenya Biodiversity Coalition*, in Nairobi, *The Grow Biointensive Agricultural Centre of Kenya (G-BIACK)*, in Thika, and *Common Ground for Africa* and *Manor House Agricultural Centre*, both in Kitale.

These photos are from their stay with G-BIACK, who CAGJ was proud to nominate for the Food Sovereignty Prize in 2011; G-BIACK was one of three groups to win Honorable Mention. Their work is highlighted in the accompanying article, *"Resistance is Fertile: Grassroots Alternatives to a Green Revolution for Africa"* by AGRA Watch Co-Chair, Janae Choquette, on p. 126.

Samuel and Peris Nderitu, founders of G-BIACK.

Samuel stands (below) with one of the center's demonstration plots. The sign reads: "Diet for one person plus income for one. Crop: local sorghum."

Our first hosts: Grow Biointensive Agricultural Center of Kenya (G-BIACK), Thika, Kenya.

Sammy, shown here, is one of the young people learning how to train farmers and provide ongoing support to them as they learn biointensive farming techniques. "Karibu" means "welcome" in Swahili.

photos this page by Heather Day

Biointensive farming is ideal for the particular challenges farmers face in Thika; it produces "the most food from the least land", restores and nourishes the soil, uses fewer resources, and can survive drought.

About G-BIACK: an amazing center for change   see p. 126

The G-BIACK center sits on one acre of land, the average size of a family farm in the region. It is designed as a model farm for small-scale farm holders. The center has over 160 double-dug beds, all planted with different types of food crops, organically grown. Soil fertility is continuously improved and maintained through the use of composted bio-matter from the center's gardens. There are also chickens, rabbits, dairy goats and an apiary. G-BIACK center staff trains small-scale farmers in sustainable ways and methods of increased food production both at our site, and through outreach to communities.

G-BIACK, the Grow Biointensive Agriculture Center of Kenya, demonstrates, trains and promotes GROW BIOINTENSIVE AGRICULTURE methods and other appropriate community development techniques for sustainability among small-scale farm holders in Central, Eastern, and Nairobi Provinces in Kenya.

G-BIACK initiatives aim at eradicating poverty and improving the living standards of resource-poor communities by promoting ecologically viable development strategies for sustainable and quality livelihoods.

(text from G-BIACK's literature)

The Grow Biointensive Agricultural Centre of Kenya (G-BIACK) is an incredible example of what can be done even with very few resources, and a taste of what could happen across the continent with more support.

This farmer is learning biointensive farming from G-BIACK. Her cows provide essential manure for her compost.

"The technologies that are promoted by the Gates Foundation in Africa are not farmer-friendly or environmentally friendly.

Some of them have not been tested fully to determine their effects on the environment and consumers.

African farmers are seeking food sovereignty, not imposed unhealthy foods and GMOs!"

—Samuel Nderitu, G-BIACK

photo by Heather Day

Tumaini Women's Group is a G-BIACK project.

This is a seed-saving workshop led by G-BIACK with the Tumaini Women's Group, whose members are widows between 70 and 102 years old, still farming, and taking care of multiple orphaned grand-children. These remarkable women are re-learning traditional techniques of saving seed.

Florence, Leader of Tumaini Women's Group, showing off her corn. She is 72 years old.

See the article *"Resistance is Fertile: Grassroots Alternatives to a Green Revolution for Africa,"* by AGRA Watch Co-Chair Janae Choquette, on p. 126.

photos this page by Travis English

Oaxaca, Mexico: 2010 Witness for Peace Delegation see p. 102

These photos come from the Witness for Peace 2010 delegation, *"Roots of Migration: Trade, Privatization, and Resistance."* They feature farmers from San Antonio, an indigenous community in Oaxaca. WFP Northwest delegates met with community leaders in Oaxaca to discuss the impacts of the North American Free Trade Agreement on rural farmers and forced migration.

For a broader context for this kind of exchange, see *"Farmers at the Table: Connecting Food and Trade Justice,"* on p. 102.

A farmer from San Juan Sosola, showing off the rich composted soil he is working on.

Delegates were humbled by the wells the San Antonio community had made with their own hands, as symbols of resistance and sovereignty in an increasingly privatized Mexico.

Witness for Peace (WFP) is a politically independent, nationwide grassroots organization of people committed to nonviolence and led by faith and conscience. WFP's mission is to support peace, justice and sustainable economies in the Americas by changing U.S. policies and corporate practices which contribute to poverty and oppression in Latin America and the Caribbean.

Toward these ends WFP Northwest has led delegations to Cuba, Mexico, and Nicaragua, most recently in 2010 and 2011.

Many of the flowers bought in the U.S. are grown in Mexico and in countries farther south.

Photos this page and bottom right, opposite page, are from a radish and flower farm in San Antonio, Oaxaca. Several generations share the labor of the farm, and cultivate a relationship with each other and with the various crops grown there.

Photos taken by CAGJ member Charity Burggraaf, on a Witness for Peace Delegation in Oaxaca, Mexico. All photos copyright Charity Burggraaf 2010.

Washington Young Farmers Coalition see p. 77

The Washington Young Farmers Coalition holds multiple educational and social events to support young and beginning farmers throughout the state. Farming and fun are main ingredients in YFC events.

photos by Kelly O

See the article *"Washington Young Farmers Cultivate Community"* by Addie Candib, on p. 77.

The Coalition connects young farmers with needed resources and opportunities for sharing knowledge, which sometimes take the form of a party! Over 200 folks showed up to the First Annual Young Farmers Mixer on Vashon Island, 2010 (shown here).

"Foley Road Orchard" (detail), by Terry Hope

Traditional Foods of Puget Sound Feed Culture, Body, & Spirit

see p. 40

To learn about the cultural renaissance happening in Indian Country around traditional foods and medicines, see Elise Krohn's article *"Traditional Foods of Puget Sound"* on p. 40.

Elise Krohn (center) leads a class in making kelp pickles at Quinault, through the Northwest Indian College's Traditional Plants Program. For Elise's recipe for kelp pickles, see p. 152.

Tribal Cooks Camp dinner with seafood chowder, clam fritters, sprouts, wild rice and bannock bread.

Squaxin Island Tribe members in western Washington harvesting camas bulbs for a traditional foods dinner. The camas prairies, an important traditional food source, once blanketed large regions of Washington State, and are being cultivated and harvested again by many tribes today.

photos by Elise Krohn

Chart detailing the enmeshed nature of the relationships and monetary and personnel ties between AGRA (Alliance for a Green Revolution in Africa) and Monsanto, the aggressive multinational biotechnology corporation. AGRA Watch is a project of CAGJ that challenges the Gates Foundation's problematic agricultural development programs in Africa, and participates in national and international organizing efforts to build community-based, agroecological solutions to hunger and climate change here, in Africa, and around the world.

See "Resistance is Fertile," p. 126.

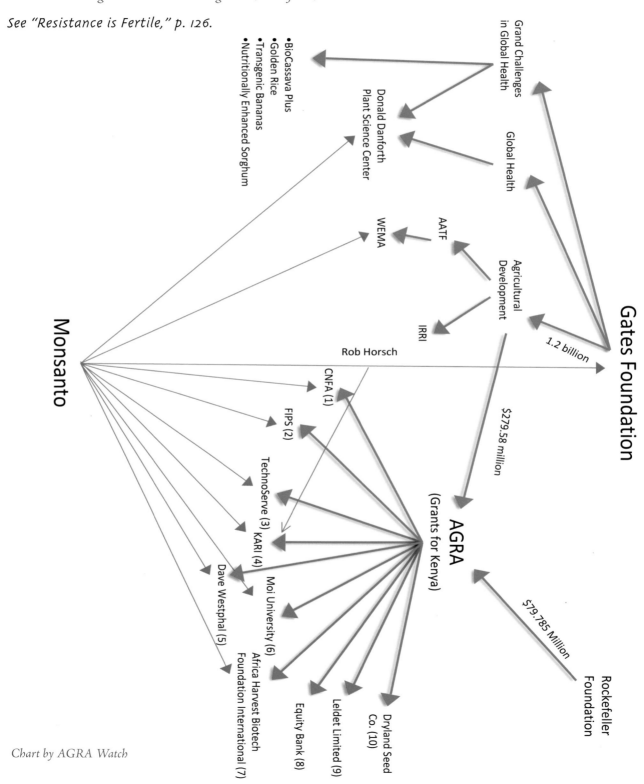

Chart by AGRA Watch

The lesson here is that more food doesn't necessarily mean less hunger. Hunger deepened in the wake of the first Green Revolution in spite of record yields. Sadly, this has been one of the lasting legacies of the Green Revolution—today enough food is produced to adequately feed 1.5 times the number of people on the planet, yet over 1 billion people are hungry.

Resource-extractive and chemical-intensive, industrial agriculture has also been a major contributor to environmental degradation that is now reaching a point of crisis. The Green Revolution severely depleted and polluted land, soil, and water; facilitated erosion and deforestation; reduced biodiversity; and undermined the ecological base on which human life depends.

It's heartening that the Gates Foundation and AGRA acknowledge some of these detrimental impacts, calling for the second Green Revolution to be "greener" than the first and emphasizing the importance of helping smallholder farmers, particularly women, rather than "supplanting them with industrial farming".

Beyond positive changes in language, however, their approach remains largely unchanged.

Overwhelmingly, AGRA and Gates Foundation grantees maintain Green Revolution practices and strategies, focusing on boosting the productivity of small-scale farmers by increasing their access to markets, inputs (improved seeds, chemical fertilizers), and credit to buy them. Though the Gates Foundation and AGRA pay lip service to agroecological methods and farmer participation, almost all of their funding goes to industrial agriculture projects and lab-based research. And the Gates Foundation openly acknowledges in its "theory of change" that its work will lead to some degree of "land mobility", a euphemism for farmers being forced out of agriculture and into other sectors (more likely joblessness, as we've seen with the first Green Revolution).

African farmers, activists, and civil society organizations are gravely concerned about what the Gates Foundation and its AGRA project are doing, and many of

> In spite of arguably good intentions, these market-driven, technology-based initiatives are actively undermining not just the possibility of alternatives, but the thousands of community-based projects that already exist in Africa.

them reject a Green Revolution for Africa. In addition to objections that AGRA was developed without consulting Africans and has since involved only a few elites (like chair of AGRA Kofi Annan) that don't represent the interests of small farmers, grassroots groups such as the Kenya Biodiversity Coalition fear the results of a second Green Revolution will be too much like the first: farmers will be dispossessed, the environment will be damaged, and food insecurity will actually increase.

> *"AGRA is poison for our farming systems and livelihoods. Under the philanthropic banner of greening agriculture, AGRA will eventually eat away what little is left of sustainable small-scale farming in Africa."*
>
> —Kenya Biodiversity Coalition

This begs the question: *Who does stand to gain from a Green Revolution in Africa?*

One of the primary beneficiaries of the first Green Revolution was the private sector. With farmers increasingly dependent on external inputs and international markets, and with a few transnational corporations mediating access to both, corporate control over world food systems has grown exponentially. It isn't difficult to see how corporations would have a vested interest in extending the Green Revolution (and all the potential for profit it represents) into Africa, especially looking at some of the activities of the Gates Foundation's grantees.

For example, several organizations funded by the Gates Foundation, including the Danforth Plant Science Center, are lobbying African governments to adopt regulatory frameworks that will allow for new seed varieties to be privatized. With these policies in place, corporations can take indigenous crops cultivated by African farmers over centuries, modify them through conventional breeding or genetic engineering, and then claim ownership of the "new" variety through patenting. This appropriation and privatization of African genetic wealth (also known as *bio-piracy*) wrests control over seed from farmers and forces them to pay for the right to use their own seeds.

Gates Foundation grantees are also pressuring African governments to pass biosafety legislation that will pave the way for GM crops to flood the continent. The legalization of GM crops throughout Africa would be highly profitable for agribusiness corporations; incidentally, biotech titan Monsanto is tied to over 70% of AGRA's grantees in Kenya (the Danforth Plant Science Center among them) and works closely with the Gates Foundation, which has spent over $200 million funding GM crop research and development in Africa since 2005.

Against this backdrop, farmers across Kenya are putting up "GMO Free Zone" signs on their land, recognizing the known and unknown risks GM crops pose to the environment, agricultural systems, and consumer safety. Genetic engineering has already been linked to superweeds, superpests, and genetic contamination of indigenous plants, while independent research has found possible links between consumption of GM crops and serious health issues. These concerns have not been sufficiently addressed by the biotech industry or regulatory bodies, but the commercialization, patenting, and distribution of GM seed continues at an alarming pace, with little public knowledge or participation.

> Farmers across Kenya are putting up "GMO Free Zone" signs on their land, recognizing the known and unknown risks GM crops pose to the environment, agricultural systems, and consumer safety.

As the systemic crisis of capital rocks the world economic system to its core, corporations are desperate to find new markets. It is clear in everything from the push for a Green Revolution, to struggles around GM crops, to massive landgrabs happening across the continent, that Africa is seen as a final frontier for agribusiness and the biotech industry to make money. The hungry themselves are seen as an important market, as evidenced by a series of reports funded by the Gates Foundation and other big corporations at the World Economic Forum in 2011. In particular, "The Next Billions: Business Strategies to Enhance Food Values Chains and Empower the Poor" seems to present the problem of food insecurity as an exciting business opportunity and encourages the private sector to target the billions of hungry and poor as one of the largest remaining untapped markets in the world. The phrase "hunger-profiteering" comes to mind.

Unfortunately, many non-profit organizations and philanthropies are leading the charge and acting as vehicles for a fundamentally corporate agenda. In spite of arguably good intentions, these market-driven, technology-based initiatives (including AGRA) are actively undermining, not just the possibility of alternatives, but also the thousands of community-based projects that already exist in Africa.

> *"The push [by AGRA] for a corporate-controlled chemical system of agriculture is parasitic on Africa's biodiversity, food sovereignty, seed and small-scale farmers…We will resist these misguided, top-down but heavily-funded initiatives from the North, which show little or no understanding or respect for our complex systems. We ask that we be allowed to define our own path forward."*
>
> —Statement on AGRA, signed by 70 African organizations
> from 12 countries, 2007 World Social Forum, Kenya

photo Heather Day

The Grow Biointensive Agricultural Centre of Kenya (G-BIACK) is an incredible example of what can be done even with very few resources, and a taste of what could happen across the continent with more support. Samuel and Peris Nderitu founded G-BIACK in 2008 in Thika, Kenya—a region that suffers some of the most difficult conditions in the country, including ongoing drought, hunger, and a high concentration of HIV/AIDS. Their beautiful center includes a community library, seed bank, classroom, and one-acre demonstration farm, where they provide on-site trainings in animal husbandry, seed-saving, water conservation, and biointensive techniques.

Biointensive farming is ideal for the particular challenges farmers face in Thika; it produces "the most food from the least land", restores and nourishes the soil, uses fewer resources, and can survive drought.

photo Travis English

photo Heather Day

The Tumaini Women's Group reached out to G-BIACK to re-learn seed saving.

Samuel Nderitu with one of the biointensive demonstration plots that are teaching farmers self-reliant and regionally appropriate farming techniques in Thika, Kenya.

In just a few years of operation, G-BIACK has trained over 6,000 farmers while supporting leaders in surrounding areas to establish their own projects. For example, after years of crop failures and growing debt from chemical agriculture brought in by foreign NGOs, the Tumaini Women's Group reached out to G-BIACK to relearn traditional ways of farming and start their own community seed bank. In this way, the work of G-BIACK has had a powerful impact far beyond its own backyard; their programs have empowered whole communities to build sustainable, resilient food systems free from corporate control—all on a shoe-string budget.

> "These developments [AGRA] claim that they bring progress to Africa. But not only will they fail to address hunger and climate change, they will make them worse. These false solutions are cynical attempts by the corporations to reach new markets, and to make a business out of a crisis."
>
> —African Biodiversity Network

> *"The technologies that are promoted by the Gates Foundation in Africa are not farmer-friendly or environmentally friendly. Some of them have not been tested fully to determine their effects on the environment and consumers. African farmers are seeking food sovereignty, not imposed unhealthy foods and GMOs!"*
>
> —Samuel Nderitu, G-BIACK
> (Grow Biointensive Agricultural Centre of Kenya)

See more of Samuel and Peris Nderitu's work with G-BIACK in the color photo section of the book.

Such "grassroots revolutions" in Africa are part of a growing international movement calling for food sovereignty and agroecological farming as solutions to hunger and climate change. They represent a wealth of alternatives to a Green Revolution for Africa, and indeed to the agricultural model that has failed farmers and consumers in the United States. As we're standing up to corporate power here, African farmers are standing up and resisting the corporate power inside the Green Revolution Trojan Horse—if we are to have any hope of taking back our food systems, we must stand together.

Janae Choquette lives and makes trouble in Seattle, WA, where she is just one of the countless amazing people working in solidarity with communities around the world to build grassroots movements for social justice.

Another World is Possible! Globalize the hope, globalize the struggle!

To learn more or get involved, please contact AGRA Watch:

agrawatch@seattleglobaljustice.org

Resources & References:

"About AGRA." Alliance for a Green Revolution in Africa. 17 Mar. 2010. www.agra-alliance.org

African Biodiversity Network. Mount Kenya Declaration on the Global Crisis and Africa's Responsibility. 31 May 2009. www.grain.org

Africa's Turn: A New Green Revolution for the 21st Century. Publication. The Rockefeller Foundation, July 2006. www.rockefellerfoundation.org

AGRA Facts. Issue Brief. Food First, 17 Sept. 2009. www.foodfirst.org

Agroecology and Sustainable Development. Issue brief. Pesticide Action Network North America, Apr. 2009. www.agassessment-watch.org

Altieri, Miguel A. Agroecology: The Science of Sustainable Agriculture. Boulder: Westview, 1995. Print.

Altieri, Miguel A. "Ecological Impacts of Industrial Agriculture and the Possibilities for Truly Sustainable Farming". Hungry for Profit: The Agribusiness Threat to Farmers, Food, and the Environment. Ed. Fred Magdoff, John Bellamy Foster, and Frederick H. Buttel. New York: Monthly Review, 2000. 77-92. Print.

Bill and Melinda Gates Foundation, 2010. "2010 Annual Report". www.gatesfoundation.org

Biotechnology and Sustainable Development. Issue brief. Pesticide Action Network North America, Aug. 2010. Web. www.panna.org

Day, Heather, and Travis English. "In Kenya, Farmers Grow Their Own Way." YES! Magazine. 4 Oct. 2010. www.yesmagazine.org/people-power/in-kenya-farmers-grow-their-own-way

De Schutter, Olivier. Report Submitted by the UN Special Rapporteur on the Right to Food. United Nations Human Rights Council, 20 Dec. 2010. www.srfood.org

English, Travis, and Philip Bereano. "Looking in a Gift Horse's Mouth." Third World Resurgence. Third World Network, Aug. 2010. www.twnside.org.sg

"Frequently Asked Questions." Alliance for a Green Revolution in Africa. 17 Mar. 2010. www. agra-alliance.org/section/about/faq

Holt-Giménez, Eric, Miguel A. Altieri, and Peter Rosset. Ten Reasons Why the Rockefeller and the Bill and Melinda Gates Foundations' Alliance for Another Green Revolution Will Not Solve the Problems of Poverty and Hunger in Sub-Saharan Africa. Issue Brief no. 12. Food First, 20 Oct. 2006. www.foodfirst.org

Holt-Giménez, Eric, Raj Patel, and Annie Shattuck. Food Rebellions!: Crisis and the Hunger for Justice. Cape Town: Pambazuka, 2009. Print.

International Assessment of Agricultural Knowledge, Science and Technology for Development. 2008. www.agassessment.org

Lappé, Frances Moore, Joseph Collins, and Peter Rosset. "Beyond Guilt and Fear" 1998. The Paradox of Plenty: Hunger in a Bountiful World. Ed. Douglas H. Boucher. Oakland: Food First, 1999. 4-71. Print.

Mayet, Mariam. Africa's Green Revolution Rolls out the Gene Revolution. Issue Brief. African Centre for Biosafety, Apr. 2009. www.biosafetyafrica.net

Mittal, Anuradha, and Melissa Moore, eds. Voices from Africa: African Farmers and Environmentalists Speak Out Against a New Green Revolution in Africa. Rep. The Oakland Institute, Mar. 2009. www.oaklandinstitute.org/voicesfromafrica/VoicesReport

Patel, Raj, Eric Holt-Giménez, and Annie Shattuck. "Ending Africa's Hunger." The Nation 21 Sept. 2009. www.thenation.com

Realizing a New Vision for Agriculture: A Roadmap for Stakeholders. World Economic Forum, 2011. www3.weforum.org

Scientists Support Farmers Regaining Control of Agriculture. Issue brief. Pesticide Action Network North America, Mar. 2010. www.panna.org

Shiva, Vandana. 1991. The violence of the green revolution: Third World agriculture, ecology, and politics. London: Zed Books.

The Next Billions: Business Strategies to Enhance Food Values Chains and Empower the Poor. World Economic Forum, 2011. www3.weforum.org

Thompson, Carol B. "How Healthy for Africans Is the Alliance for a Green Revolution?" Editorial. Pambazuka News, 361st ed. Pambazuka, 10 Apr. 2008. www.pambazuka.org

"What Bill Gates Doesn't Know About GMOs." TakePart Home. Pesticide Action Network North America, 3 Feb. 2012. www.takepart.com/article/2012/02/02/the-flip-side-what-bill-gates-doesnt-know-about-gmos

Ashley Fent

Untitled

On this trail of forgotten wisdom
a glimpse, once buried, rises
moist with dew
in the auspices of chaos
a momentary reflection
before dawn

Matthew Cronheim

Recipes:
The Food Justice Cookbook

Beverages

Appetizers

Local Entrées

Global Entrées

Desserts

Survival

These recipes come to us from all corners of the globe, from volunteers, friends, neighbors, family, allies, and compatriots, all working through the medium of food to bring people together around a common table and around our common humanity.

In our work for food justice at home and afar, sharing a meal together with love can be as powerful and radical an act as marching together, as we renew our bodies and nourish our visions for a just food future for all. In this spirit, we offer these recipes to you.

IMPORTANT NOTE ON WILD FORAGING:

Some of the recipes in this section reference wild edible plants that can be found growing throughout the Pacific Northwest. While the editors wholeheartedly endorse culinary exploration and new skills, we remind you that wild food gathering is a skill that must be acquired with the assistance of professional botanists and herbalists. This book is not intended as a guide to wild edibles, and the recipes in this cookbook should be used in combination with guidance from a certified expert on wild foods.

Beverages

Rose Hip Raspberry Soda   *Valerie Segrest*

Both youngsters and adults enjoy this refreshing fizzy beverage.

2 Tablespoons rose hips
2 cups boiling water
1 Tablespoon honey
2 cups raspberry fruit juice
2 cups sparkling water

Put loose tea in a teapot or pan and cover with boiling water. Let steep 10 minutes then add honey and stir. Allow the tea to cool and then combine strained tea with juice and sparkling water in a pitcher. Serve cold.

Prep time: 15 minutes
Serves: 4

Rose hips are high in vitamin C and are beneficial for immune health. Pick rose hips in the fall when they are orange to red. Pinch off the brown dried sepals so there is a little opening in the hip. Dry in baskets until completely dry then store in glass jars or plastic bags.

Wild Berry Tea *Elise Krohn*

This tart, delicious tea is an excellent daily brew for people with diabetes or heart disease. Huckleberry leaf helps lower blood sugar and is high in antioxidants. Rosehips and hawthorn are high in Vitamin C and bioflavenoids, that protect the heart and blood vessels. Rosehips are high in Vitamin C.

2 parts dried huckleberry leaf (red, mountain or evergreen)

1 part dried berry leaves (strawberry, raspberry, blackberry or hawthorn)

1 part dried hawthorn berry

1 part dried rose hips

1 part dried mint

***Optional - ½ part licorice root for sweetness**

Blend all ingredients. Use 1 tablespoon per cup of boiled water. Steep 15 minutes and strain. Serve straight or with sweetener.

Huckleberry leaf is high in antioxidants and helps to protect people against the side effects of diabetes. Dried berry leaves are astringent and tonic.

Wild Herbal Tea   *Brady Ryan*

Some Spruce (*Picea species*) **needles, chopped** (Young, soft light green new growth in the spring is best because you can eat it too!)

Some Lemon Balm (*Melissa officinalis*) **leaves, chopped**

Some red clover flower clusters (*Trifolium pratense*)

Some Purple Dead Nettle flower stalks (*Lamium purpureum*)

Boil water and steep ingredients, covered, for 10 minutes.

Spruce, Fir or Hemlock Tip Tea   *Elise Krohn*

In late spring the evergreen trees start to show their new leaf growth. Tiny lime-green buds appear on the tips of branches, and as the heat of the season settles in, they open up and elongate. These young tips can be eaten straight as a trail snack, put into salads, or made into tea. **Douglas fir, true fir, hemlock** *and* **spruce** *tips all have a good lemony flavor, are high in vitamin C and are very nutritious.*

Pick young evergreen tips in late springtime, when they are soft and bright green.

Ratio: One large handful of evergreen tips, to one quart of water

To make sun tea, add a large handful per quart of water to a glass container with a lid. Cover and let sit in the sun for two to six hours. Strain and serve chilled. To make hot tea use the same amount of tips to water, but pour boiled water over them in a pot and let sit 15 minutes. Strain and serve hot.

Fir tips photo © Karen Phillips 2012

143

Raspberry Rain Honey IPA *A well balanced original IPA*
Karla Makholm & Dennis van de Goor

Two years ago we decided to start brewing beer. As juniors in college we were starting to feel the pinch of buying good beer on a regular basis; long ago were the days of Budweiser, Coors and Miller Highlife. As a foodie and a Netherlander, we had developed a taste for dark, malty, hoppy and especially unfiltered beers. After spending two summers at Dennis's father's home in southern Germany, we decided there was no going back.

Being a cook on my part, and a talented scientist on Dennis's, we were confident we could make it work. Our first beer was a German Witbier with orange and coriander. It was absolutely delicious! We moved on to a Honey Blossom Lager, White Ale, Schwarzbier, Cherry Ale and an Irish Red. The beers were so tasty and full-bodied and the nutrients preserved from not filtering gave us a healthy glow. Not to mention, we were saving money.

We love sharing these delicious brews with friends and family. They make great gifts and pair well with many tasty homemade meals. Enjoy!

Rounding up the necessary equipment for brewing is fun and well worth the effort.

The Raspberry Rain Honey IPA is a well-balanced copper color IPA, with a hint of raspberry honey. The hoppy flavor is perfectly complimented by a medium bodied malt backbone.

Makes: IPA of 69-IBU; copper color. 5 gallon batch

Raspberry Rain Honey IPA

3.3 lbs light malt extra

3.3 lbs amber malt extract

1 lbs 2row pale

1 lbs crystal grain 80L

 # .5oz Columbus @ 60 min

 # .5oz Chinook @ 60 min

 # .5oz Centennial @ 60 min

 # .5oz Chinook @ 30 min

 # .5oz Cascade @ 30 min

 # .5oz Chinook @ 30 min

 # .5oz Cascade @ 0 min

 # 1oz Centennial @ 0 min

 # 1oz Chinook @ 0 min

 # 1lbs raspberry honey @ 0 min

5 oz priming sugar

dry ale yeast

6 gal water

Part I

1. *Steep crystal, wheat and pale in 2gal of (bottled) water for 30 minutes at 1558F*
2. *Strain out grain*
3. *Heat to boiling and set timer for 60 minutes while adding malt extracts*
4. *Follow hop schedule*
5. *Cool pots of wort before transferring to 5gal glass carboy*
6. *Use funnel to fill carboy with wort while straining out the remaining hops and fill with bottled water to reach 5gal*
7. *Pitch the yeast and place in cool, dark place to ferment*

Part II

1. *Dissolve corn sugar in quart of bottled water*
2. *Add cooled priming sugar solution before bottling*

photos by Karla Makholm

Before brewing: get a friend on board, consult the internet for tips on brewing and a list of equipment you will need, and if possible take a look at "The Complete Joy of Home Brewing" (we have gotten many good recipe ideas and techniques from here). Good luck!

145

Appetizers

Raw Kale Salad
Aba Ifeoma

The trick to this salad is preparing it in a stainless steel bowl. Not aluminum—check it with a magnet The magnet should stick firmly, not easily slide around. Stainless steel helps the greens break down quickly, while you toss them. Toss for about 7-10 minutes and they will be significantly more tender. NOTE: The longer the salad is in the bowl, the more tender the greens become; change bowls at your preferred tenderness. Sprinkle some pine nuts on top for texture. By all means experiment with this recipe! I toss it with different kinds of mushrooms, carrot ribbons, even quinoa. (of course it's not 100% raw if you use quinoa). Enjoy.

5 bunches of curley kale	**1/3 cup Olive oil**
1 Large onion	**¼ cup Lemon juice**
5 Cloves garlic	**3 tbs Toasted sesame seed oil**
½ cup Bragg's Amino liquid	**Cayenne pepper to taste**

Chop kale into small pieces and blend the rest of the ingredients in a food processor. Pour this liquid over the kale in a stainless bowl. Let sit two hours before serving.

Aba Ifeoma is a founding member and current treasurer of The Detroit Black Community Food Security Network (DBCFSN). The lead beekeeper at DBCFSN's D-Town Farm and the proud mother of two college students, Aba submitted this recipe at CAGJ's 2011 Annual Supporting Local Economies Everywhere (S.L.E.E.) dinner.

Smoked Salmon and Asparagus Salad

from the Columbia City Farmer's Market, Seattle

In any ratio to suit your palate:

Fresh pasta

Roasted asparagus

Smoked salmon

Fresh grated Parmesan cheese

Cook the pasta, roast the asparagus, and sprinkle the salmon, cheese and asparagus on top.

During the market season, the Columbia City Farmers Market—one of dozens around Seattle—invites some of the city's best chefs for an amazing series of free cooking demos. These demos are a unique opportunity to watch professional chefs in action right in the midst of the produce, and to learn tips and secrets to making great—and affordable—food, to inspire you to eat seasonally and help you learn more about local fruits and vegetables.

To learn more: www.seattlefarmersmarkets.org/recipes

Kale Chips *Victoria Gibson*

1 bunch of kale

2 Tablespoons olive oil

salt, pepper or other seasonings

mixing bowl

parchment paper

1. *Wash and pat dry the kale leaves, then rip or cut the kale off its stem.*
2. *Pour olive oil and seasonings in the mixing bowl.*
3. *Add the kale to the seasoning mix.*
4. *Flatten the kale as much as you can, then place on the baking pan with parchment paper.*
5. *Take out once crispy, 10–15 minutes*

Backyard Foraging: Spring Wild Salad   *Brady Ryan*

Backyard Foraging: Free Food at your Feet

On the lot of the house that I rent in Ravenna, we grow a great deal of vegetables in garden beds, but the majority of vegetation on the property are plants happily growing of their own accord, without our help or even awareness. Often, these plants are called weeds—or even invasive species (e.g. English Ivy, Butterfly Bush). However, slapping the "weed" label onto these plants only reinforces an assumption that unsown plants have nothing to offer us.

It just so happens that 20 of the 30 wild plants on my lot are fully edible, and most of the others have non-food uses. The question often arises why I grew up eating the plants growing in my vegetable beds like lettuce, spinach, broccoli, radishes, and not the plants growing around the edges such as dandelion, chickweed, sorrel, lamb's quarter's, honesty plant and wild mustard. To answer this question is to peer into a deep intertwining between the concepts of culture, food, personal tastes, edibility, class, and human control. A big undertaking! For now, I am content to put aside the question and enjoy a delicious wild salad from my backyard.

I enjoy this salad immensely because the tastes encountered are stronger and more varied than what cultivated vegetables often offer, the plants are free and can be eaten extremely fresh, and they are more resilient than my vegetables and thus are available for more of the year. But, perhaps most importantly, it is fun to make my salads and it adds spice to my life and my kitchen to seek, identify and eat these backyard wild morsels. Below is an example of an early spring wild salad I make from around my house and the close neighborhood around me. I wash it down with my Wild Herbal Tea (see Beverages) and finally, for dessert, I eat a big fresh delicious donut rescued from the dumpster of a popular donut shop in my neighborhood, because no foraged meal is complete without some truly urban foraging!

Spring Wild Salad

1 part young Chickweed (*Stellaria media*) **tops**
harvest with scissors below the growing tips, but above where the stems have gotten too stringy

1/3 part young Dandelion (*Taraxacum officinale*) **leaves**, chopped into bite size pieces, from plants that were growing in slight shade, and have yet to shoot up a flower stalk

1/3 part Nipplewort (*Lapsana communis*) **leaves**, chopped into small pieces

1/4 part Bittercress (*Cardamine species*) **rapini**; the tops of the flowering plants, with some immature seed pods

1/5 part Wild Lettuce (*Lactuca serriola*) **leaves**, chopped

1/5 part Wood Sorrel (*Oxalis species*) **or Sheep Sorrel** (*Rumex acetosella*) **leaves**

Sprinkling of Common Daisy flowers (*Bellis perennis*)

Sprinkling of Honesty Plant (*Lunaria annua*), flowers and immature seed pods

Wood Sorrel leaves & flower

Chickweed leaves & flowers

*Miner's Lettuce
(shown above & below)*

Wash all items thoroughly, dry, mix, and enjoy with simple vinaigrette. The ratios are simply to show how I try to balance different tastes like bitter, mild, pungent, sour, and others to fit my tastes. Based on your own tastes, and the season, no two wild salads will ever look the same!

A WEED IS A PLANT WHOSE VIRTUES HAVE NOT BEEN DISCOVERED.
—Ralph Waldo Emerson

Photos this page by Elise Krohn

Nettle Pesto   *Elise Krohn*

Nettles are a truly amazing wild vegetable that offers both blood cleansing and immune building properties. They are packed with essential vitamins and minerals, making just a small portion incredibly nutritious. Try tossing this pesto with pasta or baked vegetables. It can also be spread on crackers or fresh vegetables as a snack.

1 small bag (about 6 cups) **of young fresh nettles, rinsed**

1 bunch basil, stems removed, washed and drained (about 2 cups leaves)

½ cup Parmesan or Romano cheese, grated

1/3 cup walnuts or pine nuts

1/3 cup of extra virgin olive oil

1 clove garlic, chopped

1 teaspoon lemon juice

Salt and pepper to taste

Boil nettles in water (blanch) for one minute to remove the sting. Drain well, let cool and roughly chop. Place nettles, basil, nuts, cheese, olive oil, garlic and lemon juice in a food processor or blender. Blend until smooth. Add salt and pepper to taste. Place the pesto in a clean jar and pour a little extra olive oil over the top. Cover with a lid. This will keep for 2-3 weeks in the refrigerator.

Cook time: 10 minutes

Kelp Pickles   *Elise Krohn*

Gather kelp by pulling it up when in a boat, or gather fresh-looking kelp off the beach after a storm. If the outer skin is tough, remove it with a vegetable peeler. Chop up the end bulb and the tail into small pieces. Place in clean glass jars. Combine remaining ingredients in a pan and bring to a boil. Pour over the sliced kelp and close lids tight. When cooled, refrigerate.

Wait one week before eating.

- **1 fresh bull whip of kelp**
- **2 cups vinegar**
- **1 cup water**
- **1 tablespoon salt**
- **2 cloves garlic, minced**
- **1 Tablespoon pickling seasoning**

Miguel Hernandez harvests bull kelp on the Strait of Juan de Fuca, 2012.

Kelp is packed with minerals and is considered a medicine to many families. It has a distinctive salty flavor that lends itself well to pickling. These crunchy treats can be used in salads or eaten straight.

Photos this page by Elise Krohn

151

Dandelion Drop Biscuits   *Elise Krohn*

My husband was delighted to find something tasty that we can do with all those flowering dandelions in our yard! This recipe is quick, easy and completely satisfying.

2 cups all purpose flour

2 and ½ teaspoons baking powder

½ teaspoon of salt

1 teaspoon dried herbs, such as rosemary, marjorum, thyme, basil or chive

5 tablespoons cold unsalted butter, cut into small pieces

1 cup milk

½ cup dandelion flowers—pulled off the base

Preheat oven to 450°. Mix all ingredients by hand so butter is the consistency of coarse bread crumbs. Do not let butter melt. Do not overwork. Batter should be moist and sticky but not smooth. Use a spoon to form about ¼ cup scoops. Place a couple inches apart. Bake until the bottom is browned and the edges are just starting to brown, about 12 minutes.

Dandelion petals put to good use!

Entrées: Local & Global

Salmon Wrapped in Skunk Cabbage *Elise Krohn*

a traditional Coast Salish preparation for cooked salmon

Skunk cabbage leaves are also called "Indian wax paper," because they are used for drying and wrapping different foods. When they are used in cooking, they impart a sweet taste to the dish. Wrapping salmon like this preserves the healing oils in the fish. You can find skunk cabbage leaves in swampy areas. Gather medium sized leaves when they are still tender.

This recipe was inspired by Rudolph Rÿser (Cowlitz) of the Center for World Indigenous Studies.

4 salmon steaks

4-6 skunk cabbage leaves

2 Tbsp wild onion bulb & leaves, chopped

    (or 2 cloves garlic, minced)

Salt and pepper

Wash, and if the center of the leaf is rigid, let the leaves sit in hot water to soften them. Place a salmon steak in the center of a skunk cabbage leaf. Sprinkle with salt, pepper and a little chopped wild onion or garlic. Fold the leaf around the salmon so it is completely covered. Use two leaves if necessary.

Finish the rest of the steaks and place them in a deep rectangular baking dish with a tight-fitting lid. Place a little water in the base of the pan. Cover and bake at 350° for about 30 minutes or until the salmon is cooked. You can also cook the salmon wraps over coals on a fire. Unwrap and discard the skunk cabbage leaf.

Photos these pages by Elise Krohn

Grandma's Steamed Lemon Fish

Gladys Mercer Aitchison & family

Gladys Mercer Aitchison (born 1904) grew up in British Columbia, spending most of the summer at her family's vacation home at White Rock. Family lore has it that this is her own recipe, and was always a favorite of her husband and daughters. Gladys was a noted master of plant and herb lore, and often added foraged herbs to add to this dish.

This recipe works as well or even better with Halibut, and is wonderful prepared both in the oven, over a grill, or over a bonfire. Instructions are for the oven; if you are cooking on grill or fire you will need to open and re-seal the foil periodically, to check for doneness. Thanks to Mary Camezon from her son Phil Bevis for helping keep this recipe alive through the years. We hope you enjoy it.

The basics:

1 or more salmon or halibut fillets
1 juicy lemon per 1.5 lb of fillet (which serves 3)
1 lemon per 1.5 lb fillet, sliced thinly
2 green onions per fillet, chopped
Worcestershire sauce

Options (any or all of the following):

fresh zucchini, cut into match sticks
cherry tomatoes
whole spinach leaves, washed and dried
dry white wine

1. *Preheat oven to 350°*
2. *Make a boat of aluminum foil (to retain juices)*
3. *Wash salmon and place in foil—scales down*
4. *Cover top of fillet with fresh lemon slices and chopped onions*
5. *Squeeze lemons on top (with as much pulp as you can!)*
6. *Shake Worcestershire sauce on top—8 light splashes per lb of fillet*
7. *Add optional matchstick zucchini or whole cherry tomatoes*
8. *A strong urging is to add the optional wine, 1/4 cup per lb of fillet, but do not pour on top of the fish, pour around it*
9. *Cover with a tented second piece of foil, and crimp around the edges to form a seal (important as this dish steams to cook)*

One great option is to cook the fish on a bed of spinach, which will cook along with the fish for an instant and savory side dish.

Cooking times: 15 to 20 minutes is average, depending on your oven and the thickness of the fillet. A good average is 18 minutes.

Keep the juices to pour over the fish—and anything you serve with it!

Hearty Nettle Nutmeg Soup   *Annie Brulé*

This soup is rich green and delicious—for fans of cream of broccoli soup, this will open up a whole new world of taste. Serve it over rice or quinoa, or on its own as an entrée with thick slabs of fresh bread. There's no actual cream in this soup, but it takes its smoothness from the starch of the potatoes. Thanks to Elise Krohn, Joyce LeCompte-Mastenbrook, and all the friends whose nettle soups have inspired this one. There are many variations, and they are all delicious.

one large onion, roughly chopped

chopped cloves from one whole small bulb of garlic

two Tablespoons olive oil or butter

one large potato, chopped, (or) **two handfuls of un-cooked rice**—anything to add some starch or extra body to the soup; a cup of cooked grain will do as well

one large grocery bag's worth of fresh nettle tops, blanched*

four quarts of veggie, chicken, or nettle broth

1/4 teaspoon ground coriander

small dash of ground nutmeg

salt and pepper to taste

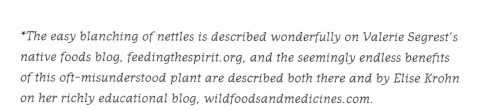

The easy blanching of nettles is described wonderfully on Valerie Segrest's native foods blog, feedingthespirit.org, and the seemingly endless benefits of this oft-misunderstood plant are described both there and by Elise Krohn on her richly educational blog, wildfoodsandmedicines.com.

When I was a small girl growing up in the woods of the Pacific Northwest, my mother would take me and my sister on walks, and show us the different plants that were edible, poisonous, friendly, and prickly. There were no bad plants, she said, just plants that took more patience to learn from. My earliest plant teacher was nettle, who teaches us patience and gentleness, despite its stinging spines. Mom taught my five year old self how to approach nettles with good intentions, and to make friends with a plant before trying to harvest anything. When treated with kindness (and when grasped only in certain places!) the spines will not sting you, and you can harvest nettles without gloves.

I strongly recommend gloves for your nettle harvest, as they'll be sure and get some stings in even with the greatest of care. The spines hold their sting until they have been heated—either by boiling or by drying in the oven. You can also hang them to dry. After being boiled or dried, the sting is gone and they are ready for eating or making nutritious tea.

For a little about nettle's incredible health attributes, see p. 150.

Preparation:

Sautée the onions and garlic in olive oil on med-high heat in the bottom of a soup pot, adding the nutmeg and coriander when the onions are just translucent, to release the spices' flavor in the oil.

Add the potato or grain to the sautée mixture, then pour in the stock and the blanched nettles (if you have previously frozen your nettles, three or four fist-sized balls of frozen nettles will do well).

Turn the heat down to med-low and simmer for about 1/2 hour until the potatoes or grain are soft. Purée the whole lot in a blender or other device (immersion blenders work beautifully). Add salt and pepper to taste.

Lasagna with Spinach

Teri C. Gibson

The first time I made lasagna, I was newly married and adventurous. I had eaten lasagna at restaurants and thought they tasted really good. I decided to make my own lasagna and that's when I learned to design lasagna to my taste and eating style. If you are vegan, you can substitute the meat with mushrooms. One of our family favorites: hamburger, half pound sausage, pound of mushrooms, and layer with spinach. There is no end to the possibilities of the type of lasagna you can make. You are only limited by your imagination. I hope your enjoy the experience of making lasagna.

1 box of Lasagna Noodles

½ pound of Ground Beef (or your favorite meat)

1 lb of Mushrooms

1 large jar (32 ounces) **of thick Spaghetti Sauce**

1 large container of Ricotta Cheese

1 tablespoon of Powdered Garlic (or you can use **Fresh Garlic**: 4 Garlic Cloves, cut into very small pieces)

1/3 cup grated **Parmesan Cheese**

1/3 cup of **Dry Cilantro** or 1 cup of **Fresh Cilantro,** cut into very small pieces

1 or 2 eggs

½ teaspoon of **Pepper**

½ teaspoon of **Salt**

1 pound package of Mozzarella Cheese

Half pound of Fresh Spinach.

1. Boil the lasagna noodles in a 5 quart pot
2. Brown the beef in a skillet.
3. Add the mushrooms & spaghetti sauce to the browned beef.
   Set aside. No need to cook.
4. **Ricotta Mix**: Stir Ricotta cheese, parmesan cheese, garlic,
   cilantro, eggs in a medium sized bowl. Add the pepper and salt and stir.
5. Get a roasting pan, large. Layer the bottom of the pan with the cooked noodles.
   Then layer on top of the noodles the mozzarella cheese. Next spread the Ricotta Mix
   on top of the mozzarella cheese. Pour half of your meat mixture.
6. Lay Spinach on top of the meat mixture.
7. Layer the cooked noodles, mozzarella, Ricotta Mix & the rest of the meat mixture.
8. Sprinkle Grated Parmesan Cheese on top of the meat mixture.
9. Cover pan with aluminum foil
10. Place pan in the oven, at 425°. Let cook for about 45 min. or until cheese is melted.
11. Let set for about 20 minutes, then serve.

You can make this less fattening by making the following changes:

   1 egg instead of 2
   Spaghetti sauce without sugar
   Low fat Ricotta Cheese
   Low Fat Mozzarella Cheese

For vegetarians, omit the beef and use 1 pound to 1½ pounds of mushrooms.

This lasagna is delicious with salad and your favorite drink. Enjoy!

Tsimmes & Holkes *an Ashkenazi Jewish sweet vegetable stew*

Deborah Hyman

Tsimmes and Holkes

Start with the Tsimmes:

- **3 bunches carrots,** peeled & sliced
- **1.5 lbs *flanken* (beef short rib)**
- **2 or 3 sweet potatoes,** peeled & quartered

- **1/2 cup mixed white & brown sugar**
- **prunes and/or raisins** (optional)
- **salt to taste**

Put ingredients in large pot. Add water to cover
Simmer gently approximately 30 minutes

Add Holkes:

- **2 large potatoes,** roughly grated
- **Matza meal**—enough to make mixture hold together
- **Salt and pepper**
- **One-quarter cup chicken fat** (or substitute **margarine)**

Form above ingredients into 4 large balls, and disperse balls into simmering carrots.
Continue to simmer approximately 30 more minutes, basting holkes as they cook.

Drain liquid.
Mix small amount of maple syrup and/or molasses into carrots/sweet potatoes.
Transfer to casserole dish and bake at 325° for about one hour.

This tsimmes has been served at Passover Seder meals at my great-grand-father's tenement flat in the north end of Hartford, at my aunt and uncle's spacious colonial home in the Connecticut suburbs, and in a cohousing com-mon house dining room in British Columbia.

Family lore has it that this recipe is my great-grandfather's, brought from Bialystok, Ukraine in 1900 when he emigrated to America at the age of 19. We went to Passover Seders at his flat, where long tables were lined up through the living and dining rooms to accommodate the extended families of his seven children. But I didn't know he could cook. I only learned that when my father decided to try making the tsimmes for Passover shortly after Papa Louie died. My father said he remembered Papa Louie—his pater-nal grandfather—making the dish years earlier, before he turned over that responsibility to his wife and daughters as his livelihood grew from a single horse-drawn fruit and vegetable cart to a thriving produce wholesale busi-ness.

My father brought the tsimmes to our suburban Seders with a mix of trepi-dation and pride and a hint of challenge toward his older sister, my Aunt Rita. He agonized over proportions of carrots to sweet potatoes; he accused his sister of sabotaging him by not heating the tsimmes thoroughly; he var-ied the recipe—meatless, with prunes, with raisins, with golden raisins; and he claimed every year to have ruined the dish in one way or another. More white sugar than brown didn't taste right. The holkes [potato dumplings] didn't stay together. The carrots were too soft and the sweet potatoes were still hard.

Nevertheless, each year the tsimmes was the main attraction of the meal, outshining the turkey and the kosher-for-Passover trimmings. The tsimmes was served in a deep casserole dish, the lid raised ceremoniously to reveal a stew the oranges and yellows of carrots and sweet potatoes, dotted with the black and gold of raisins and the crusty brown edges of the half-buried holkes. The one year my father skipped making tsimmes, and we brought steamed asparagus to the Seder instead, has never been forgiven or forgotten.

The tsimmes recipe came west with me, typed on a half-sheet of paper that is by now yellowed and spattered. I am most proud of having served it at a Passover Seder gathering in the common house dining room at WindSong Cohousing in Langley, British Columbia, where my daughters spent their formative childhood years, and holidays were an opportunity to share one's cultural traditions with the rest of the community.

Tsimmes recipe thanks to Louis Hyman, born Bialystok, Ukraine 1882, died Hartford, CT 1973.

Cooling Mung Bean Soup *Kay Yu Yuan Chai*

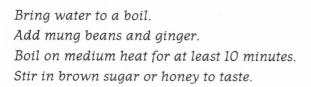

Mung bean soup has been traditionally used by Chinese to reduce heat and cool down the body especially during the summer. Not only that, it is also consumed to detoxify the liver. Mung bean soup is usually eaten in the late afternoon as a snack or dessert.

Raw ginger, around 3 or 4 3" slices (optional)

¼ cup mung beans

Brown sugar/honey/any sweetener to taste

1-2 cups water

Bring water to a boil.
Add mung beans and ginger.
Boil on medium heat for at least 10 minutes.
Stir in brown sugar or honey to taste.

*This recipe is incredibly versatile. You can increase water or beans according to your liking.

Boiling: Longer or Shorter?

For detoxification of the liver, boil until the beans are completely softened and eat the beans with the soup. For cooling down, boil for at least 10 minutes and drink only the soup (hard beans aren't tasty!) because the softer the beans, the longer they have been cooked, the lesser the heat reduction properties (and the better for detoxification).

Ginger: Raw or Dry Roasted?

Contrary to popular belief, ginger by itself is not warming. Its warming properties only work when it is dry roasted. Raw ginger boiled in water is incredibly cooling, whereas dry roasted ginger boiled in water has its famous warming properties. Use dry roasted ginger in the mung bean soup to balance out its extremely cooling properties and to get its detoxifying benefit without stomach upsets.

To dry roast ginger, simply roast it in a pan for 1-2 minutes, or even less, without oil until the ginger is dehydrated.

Desserts

Alison's Olive Oil Carrot Cake   *Alison Dagger*

250 ml olive oil

230 g sugar

4-5 eggs

250g flour

2 tsp baking soda

2 tsp baking powder

2 tsp cinnamon or spice mix (1 tsp cloves)

1 tsp cardamom

1 tsp salt

125 g seeds and raisins

500 g carrots

1. *Preheat oven to 170° C*

2. *Grease and flour a 10" cake pan*

3. *In a small bowl mix the wet ingredients together*

4. *In a big bowl mix the dry ingredients together*

5. *Next mix the wet mixture into the dry*

6. *Finally fold the shredded carrots, seeds and raisins into the batter*

7. *Gently pour batter into greased and floured cake pan*

8. *Bake for around 40–60 minutes.*

Wild Berry Crisp   *Elise Krohn*

This tasty dessert boasts fillings of antioxidant rich fruit and is topped with heart-healthy oats and nuts. Just thinking of potential combinations of fruit filling is deliciously satisfying. Try making a double batch and storing half in the freezer for another wild berry crisp day. It can go straight from the freezer to the oven.

Filling:

6-8 cups of berries (strawberry, huckleberry, blackberry, blueberry or a combination)

½ cup of honey, agave nectar or **xylitol,** as sweetener

2 Tablespoons corn starch (or) **1/4 cup all-purpose flour**

1 teaspoon of lemon zest (or) **two teaspoons of lemon juice**

Topping:

½ cup all purpose flour or barley flour

1½ cups rolled oats

½ cup chopped walnuts

½ cup chopped hazelnuts

2 tablespoons butter

½ cup honey, agave nectar or rice syrup

1/8 teaspoon sea salt

½ teaspoon cinnamon

Preheat oven to 375 degrees. Mix the filling ingredients and spread evenly in a 9 by 12 inch baking pan. Roast flour, oats and chopped nuts by stirring them in a dry skillet over medium heat until they are heated through and are just beginning to brown. Remove from heat and place in a bowl. Heat butter and honey, then pour over the dry mix. Add salt and cinnamon. Mix well and drop evenly over the berries. Bake for 30-40 minutes or until the berries bubble and the topping is crisp.

Cook time: 1 hour

Serves: 8-10

Guyanese Black Cake
Sue Faria

I was introduced to Black Cake almost 40 years ago by my wonderful mother-in-law, Stella Maria Faria. She and her family had emigrated to Canada from Guyana and of course brought with them their traditional dishes. I lived in Guyana for a few years just after I married. Back then I always believed Black Cake to be a Portuguese tradition (since the family I married into were Portuguese Guyanese). Not so. I later discovered that it was definitely born in the West Indies and everyone made it there.

I recognised Black Cake immediately as my English Plum pudding with the brandy substituted with good West Indian rum. However, unlike plum pudding, which is only offered as a Christmas dessert, Black Cake is made and baked for any celebration including weddings, birthdays, christenings, and yes, funerals too. I was spurred on by Stella to continue the tradition and it rapidly became the centre of attraction for each and every Christmas at home.

Here's the recipe. This fruit mixture needs to be started at least six weeks before you want to bake the cake, and you need to bake the cake at least a month before you want to eat it.

For the Fruit Mixture:

- **1 lb raisins**
- **1 lb currants,**
- **1 lb prunes** (stoned and chopped)
- **Half lb of mixed peel**

All these dried fruits are mixed and soaked in a 75cl bottle of good West Indian rum and a 75cl bottle of cheap sherry (preferably Spanish). Put that all to 'set' in an airtight container for at least six weeks.

Prepare six to eight 6" cake tins, and line with parchment paper.
(Mine are only about an inch and a half deep)

For the cake mixture:

10 eggs, lightly beaten

1lb butter

1lb demerara sugar, creamed together with the
butter, not too vigorously

1 Tablespoon cinnamon

4 Tablespoons gravy browning

Half a pound floured cherries (chopped)

1 lb good quality flour

Method:

Place the fruit mixture into a large mixing bowl—I use a plastic bucket, so much easier to get to grips with! Add the creamed sugar and butter, and mix. Gradually add the eggs and flour alternately (very important, to prevent curdling) and mix well. I always use a wooden spoon or my hands, to get an even texture. Add the remaining ingredients and mix well. Divide the mixture into each baking tin and place in a slow oven i.e. around 130° C. Depending on different ovens, baking time can take from 8 to 12 hours. If you're unsure, check often—there's no chance of ruining the cakes—and test with a skewer, which if cooked should show the merest sign of cake. When done, the cakes will have shrunk slightly from the rim.

Cool and turn out onto a platter. Fork each cake and pour a little rum over it. Wrap each one, first in cling film and then in foil, and store in a cool place—not the fridge—for at least a month. Enjoy!

NOTES:

I know you can buy mixed peel in Canada so I'm sure Americans will be familiar with it. It's usually with the baking ingredients e.g. flour, dried fruit, baking powder. The cherries (which incidentally are glacé—pronounced glas-SAY) are cherries chopped and floured. Any brown sugar will do if Demarara is not on the shelf.

continued...

The Ritual of Making Black Cake

I love the ritual of "setting" the fruit—soaking it in a potent mix of alcohol (an expensive Caribbean rum and a cheap Sherry are best) and always at "half term" when my children are on their break from school. Having said that, anytime after summer is fine but the longer the alcohol soaks in the better! That's a personal ceremony, but the mixing was always a party! I remember Jolly (my son) and his best friend Rob, Jodie, my then toddler granddaughter (now 15!), my best friends Vanessa and Sam, other friends and neighbours, cats and dogs all taking part in the mixing and prepping of the cakes. I used to leave the fruit soaking in a dark cupboard under the stairs and I'd find the kids sneaking in to smell the mixture and take a peek, months before it was ready to bake.

Nowadays I happily continue to make several cakes for each Yuletide, always for my expectant family (along with the Christmas Ham), but more for my close friends who know if they receive that round heavy fragrant present that they must be on my A list! After 35 years of baking Black Cake, I still get a buzz (could be the alcohol) but I think even as an Anglophile I make a great authentic cake along with the English greats of mushy peas, fish pie (well, any kind of pie) and of course Yorkshire puddings.

My Guyanese in-laws who moved to Canada have adapted their recipes for the cake, sometimes by experimenting with different fruit, or alcohols, cutting down considerably on the browning (therefore no longer "black" Black Cake)—and even baking them in tiny muffin trays. Their versions are tasty, but far removed now from the dense, rich and often-breathtaking slabs of cake Stella used to make. And what can I say, I'm a creature of habit and I would never dream of adulterating this wonderful, unique favourite of our family. I get so much joy making Black Cake just the way it has always been made.

—Sue Faria

Chocolate Beet Cake   *Celina Yarkin*

2 to 2 ½ cups pureed beets (steam or boil first)

1 ½ cups sugar

½ cup oil

1 tsp vanilla

½ tsp salt

1 ½ cups flour

¾ cups cocoa

2 tsp baking powder

1 ½ tsp baking soda

Mix wet ingredients and sugar and salt together. Sift together flour, baking powder, baking soda and cocoa. Add wet mix to dry, stir. Bake in a 9" round pan at 450 degrees for 45 minutes. Eat with friends!

Seven years ago, our family traveled to Hawaii, where we stayed with some friends for a few days. They have three daughters, and adhere to a vegan diet, so out of necessity and talent, Sarah is an extraordinary cook. From that trip we took away two recipes that have become a part of how we eat, and who we are. One of those is this chocolate beet cake, which I make every year for Joe's birthday, and then a bunch of times in between.... If it isn't beet season, we substitute yogurt or apple sauce. You could use carrots, or anything really, but nothing has quite the color or beets.

Now whoever chooses to read these words, and let the recipes climb onto their shelves and into their pantries, they too will be forever changed.

—Celina Yarkin

Ambulo

Abdi Isaak

From IFO refugee Camp, Daadab, Kenya— *Here is 'AMBULO' recipe. Ambulo is the food of choice for my family for about 20 years now since our government collapse in February 1990 and we fled our farm in Bardheere town located on the banks of Juba River, Somalia.*

Corn provides energy and lots of fiber while beans represent the best choice of protein in absence of meat in the refugee camps. Iodize salt is added to taste.

This is the recipe for most of us who pass through refugee camps in North Eastern Kenya. For about 20 years now, Somali refugees get beans, corn and some oil. The only food that sustained us for twenty years, though meager, is this simple and somewhat balanced mixture we called "AMBULO" in Somali language. Please share it with someone who wants to try.

Thank you. My sister, Farhiya, who is now preparing Ambulo, contributed to the part about preparation.

—Abdi Isaak

Lunch for a family of four can be prepared from:

Ingredients:
beans, maize (corn) and iodized salt, cooked in water.

(please note: these are the only ingredients available here in the refugee camps, but you can add anything as you wish)

Ambulo

1. One of cup of beans
2. One cup of corn (maize)
3. Six cups of water
4. Small amount iodized salt
5. Two table spoon oil (any kind is OK)

Preparation

Boil the water in a cooking pot.
Wash and add corn to the boiling water and let it cook for five minutes.
Add washed beans and cook for about 30 minutes on a medium heat until the maize is tender.
Any kind of oil/fat can be added now.
Cool it but serve warm.

Mail can get to us through:
world red cross mailstop.

Abdi Isaak
C14, IFO refugee camps,
C/o UNHCR
Daadab, Kenya.

Daadab is the world's largest refugee camp, with over 450,000 residents in 2012, according to the UNHCR. This photograph, taken at the Daadab airfield, shows deliveries of supplies and equipment provided by the US DoD. Photo by Tech. Sergeant Steve Staedler, U.S. Air Force.

Breaking Bread

Merna Ann Hecht

> *I believe poetry, like bread is for everyone*
> *....in the unanimous blood of those who struggle*
> **Roque Dalton**

I don't know much about the bread
that Abdi, Farah and Hodan,
my students from Somalia eat,

I don't know what ingredients are kneaded
into the dough of their survival,
I don't even know if it's flatbread or risen.

Farah writes how once he put his ear
to a road in Mogadishu
and heard an aria,
how he can still see children
playing a jumping game
caught in a leaping moment
lifted from the sad streets.

Hodan says her blood is lost
because it still belongs to the flag
of her Somali star.

Abdi tells me his mother
has sworn him to secrecy,
how his father has already used
an entire month's earnings
to surprise him
with what will be his first
suit, for graduation,
Abdi, whose heart
is like a beautiful fruit,

tender and exposed,
who tells me he believes
this is an America
that will allow him to become
a lawyer for truth
and justice, even a judge.

Children of goats milk, red dust, stringy chicken,
scarcity of grain and water,
you tell me even the Somali wind
that once sang your lullabies
is a cutthroat wanderer
who drifts in each night
with his blood smell of tribal battle.

Thinking of Somalia, brown hands over open fires,
bread shared in a circle of wizened eyes,
hungers beyond my imagining,
my thoughts leap to a restaurant table
in Seattle, though it could be San Francisco,
Sun Valley, Aspen, New York, with a waiter
who says "My name is Josh
 and I'll be your server tonight,"
where the privileged dip
foccacia or ciabatta
in olive oil infused with balsamic,
read the novellas
that menus have become,
assure themselves the eggs are local,
the cheese artisan, the ostrich organic.

What if the next fad pulls
its self important palette
away from local gardens,

and organic foods
featuring food from war zones
packaged for the hungers
of the well fed.
Goat meat from Somalia,
a pilaf or pounded grain from Sudan,
Iraqi dates covered with bitter
chocolate,
it could happen,
it could happen that the bread
of struggle will be sold
as the empathy of eating.

I want to tell Farah, Hodan and Abdi
that I know about chickens,
how they lay eggs warm in the hand,
with yolks that are simply determined
truths of yellow,
that I am not impressed
with the notion of slow food
because many of us already know
whatever is at high speed is dangerous,
and we don't need Josh
to tell us what the old Somali or Iraqi farmers'
hands have been doing for centuries,

and that I wish Abdi could become a judge
and that good bread and its unanimous communion
would be what we learn to break together.

175

This page & overleaf: Ashley Fent

Resources: Your Toolshed
for reclaiming your food system

DIY Food Growing: Building Healthy Soil

Lisa Taylor

An Excerpt from "Your Farm in the City,"
by Lisa Taylor & the gardeners of Seattle Tilth

Here at Seattle Tilth, we know there is a big difference between dirt and soil. Dirt is what you wash off your car or your hands. Soil is alive. It is filled with living things and supports other living things, such as plants, animals, and people.

Soil is a living thing, so we need to care for it as we care for all living things. I know I wouldn't thrive if I were walked on or didn't get anything to eat. One of the first lessons we teach in the Seattle Tilth Children's Garden is that, in a garden, people and plants don't belong in the same place. When we step on the soil, we compact it, squishing out space for air, water, roots, and creatures. So watch where you step.

Children in the Garden: Where Are Your Feet?

If your children will be helping cultivate and care for your city farm, take time to teach them how to be in the garden. A garden is different from being at the park or playing in the yard. In a garden, people and plants don't go in the same place. Plants live in the soil. People can walk on the grass, sidewalk, stepping-stones, and garden paths. Remind each other as often as needed to "watch your feet" or ask, "Where are your feet?"

Your Soil

What is soil? Think of it as a pie. One-half of your soil is space for air and water. Almost all of the other half (45 percent) is inorganic matter—sand, silt, clay, and rocks. Just a little slice (2–5 percent) of your soil is organic matter. This is a small piece that makes the difference between dirt and soil. It is also the glue that holds it all together and the engine that makes plants grow.

This small slice of the pie is filled with living things, including plants, animals, and microorganisms. In a teaspoon of good garden soil, there are more than 3 billion microorganisms. The smell of the forest floor is really the microorganisms—dirt alone doesn't have a smell. These tiny creatures make the difference between dirt and soil. Micro-organisms make minerals and nutrients in the soil and air available to plants. In return, plants give the microbes the energy they need to live. Without these microbes, your plants can't utilize the nutrients in your soil.

Many current landscaping practices overlook feeding the living part of the soil. In the woods, plants don't need to be fertilized or mulched. Nature is messy. Plants are designed to break apart, constantly dropping pieces of organic matter, which decompose and feed other plants. At some point we started to apply our housekeeping aesthetic to our landscapes. We are always raking up and removing leaves and other plant debris. Though I like a tidy house, I don't expect that level of cleanliness from my landscape.

Plant debris is food for the creatures in the soil. Decomposers, such as worms and sow bugs, change leftover organic material into rich humus that feeds the plants. These bits also create a carpet that suffocates weeds, eliminating competition for water, soil, and nutrients. This mulch layer helps to hold water, protects roots, and provides habitat for the microorganisms that help plants grow. It's beautiful and simple. When we try to keep our landscapes unnaturally tidy, we rob our soil of the food that makes for a healthy, vibrant ecosystem. Without organic matter, we just have dirt.

179

Soil is living and needs the same things as other living things, including the following:

SUN. There are places in your yard that get more sun and other places that are shady.

AIR. Depending on your soil type, there might be big air spaces or tiny air spaces. You can increase these spaces by loosening the soil by digging.

WATER. The water in your soil will change depending on the season and your soil type.

FOOD. What does your soil eat? Typically, other living things, like leaves, twigs, and dead insects.

Microbial Magic: At the Root Zone

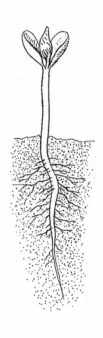

Plants can only anchor themselves in dirt. They can't make use of any mineral nutrients without the help of some really cool fungi. There is an area around the root zone where mycorrhizal fungi gather and bring minerals from the soil in a form that plants can use. The plants return the favor by giving the fungi carbohydrates. This is an amazing symbiosis that benefits both the plant and the fungi. Since these fungi help plants absorb mineral nutrients from the soil, many gardeners inoculate their beds with mycorrhizal fungi before they plant. You can get dried mycorrhizal fungi through sources online.

Compost

Building healthy soil is surprisingly easy. If you want to grow strong plants that taste great and resist pests and diseases, add compost. How do you improve heavy clay soil? Add compost. Want to make your soil retain water better, so plants don't dry out? Add compost. Compost really is a miracle worker. It boosts the health of soil, helps plants combat disease and pests, and helps conserve water. In this section you'll learn how to use the organic matter on your site to improve your soil. You'll also learn different techniques for composting yard and food waste, mulching, and growing your own fertilizer using cover crops.

Using Compost to Improve the Soil

As I've mentioned, the best way to improve soil is to add compost. If you don't have time to make your own, you can buy commercial compost in bags or have it delivered in larger quantities to use in your garden. This is a great way to start building healthy soil.

Add Compost

Measure the area you'll be working with and determine how deep you will spread the compost. Then do the math to figure out how much compost you'll need (see table). Since compost does not have high levels of nitrogen, it will not "burn" your plants, so you can plant immediately after you add it to your garden beds.[3]

- For new garden beds, mix 2 to 4 inches of compost into the top 8 to 12 inches of soil.

- To improve established garden beds, dig 1 to 2 inches of compost into the top 8 to 12 inches of soil.

- Topdress with 1 to 2 inches of compost around your perennial shrubs and in existing beds where it is impossible to mix in the compost. Topdressing means to spread a thin layer of compost on top of the soil. As you water your garden, the nutrients in the compost filter down, improving your soil. Topdressing is easy and looks great.

Lisa Taylor is the Education Program Manager for Seattle Tilth. She is a co-author of the Maritime Northwest Garden Guide and a frequent speaker on soils, compost, edible landscaping, and children's gardening. She facilitates trainings for teachers and others interested in schoolyard gardening and is passionate about teaching children and their parents where their food comes from and how to care for living things. She lives in Seattle, Washington.

DIY Food Preservation:
an Introduction to Canning & Preserving

Laura Brady

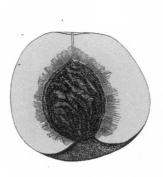

Two generations back, canning wasn't a special skill; it was a basic part of maintaining the household, wedged into its natural place between spring-cleaning and the autumn pumpkin harvest.

Since then, with the advent of cheap, commercially canned food and fruit shipped in easily from far away during the winter, canning has slipped from being considered 'normal' to, all too often, 'dangerous' and 'unsanitary.'

But the most important thing to remember is that if you follow the rules, strap on your seatbelt, watch some experts, and keep your eyes on the target, canning can be safe and lots of fun.

Food preservation has some great benefits:

It's cheap! Because you're buying fruits and vegetables (or harvesting them) at their peak locally, they're a lot less expensive that at other times of the year. If you buy them in bulk, or buy 'seconds,' you can save a lot too.

It has a low impact on the planet! If you buy your produce locally and in season, preserve it, and then eat it in the winter, you won't be supporting the high-carbon economy of eating fruit from across the globe in January.

It supports your local food economy! When you buy canned food, most of the time, you have no idea who grew those tomatoes. How much more fun is it to tell your relatives over Thanksgiving dinner, "Rose, my favorite farmer, grew these blueberries on her local farm!"

It tastes better! When you buy those canned tomatoes off the shelf in the grocery chain, they were likely grown in Mexico, cooked in Florida, canned in the Midwest, labeled in Texas, and then trucked to you as Stewed Tomatoes. Yuck! Nothing can really compare to the delightful taste of food you can or preserve at home.

Why do so many people think food preservation is dangerous?

Mostly, it's a misconception. If you follow some basic guidelines, it can be completely safe!

Let's break down what food preservation is all about:

When you preserve food, you're killing or neutralizing the naturally occurring agents that normally cause food to spoil. You can do this by freezing, heating, or simply creating an environment that is inhospitable to them. Here are the basics you should know about the food-spoiling agents:

Enzymes are present in all living things and cause decomposition. Refrigeration slows down food decomposition because enzymes only really get active between 85-120 °F. You can get rid of enzymes by heating food to 140 °F.

Molds are fungi that grow out of spores that alight naturally on foods. Some mold is good, and purposefully introduced (think of blue cheese). Other mold is not so yummy. Molds flourish between

50-100 °F. To destroy the unwanted types, heat foods to 140-190 °F. The higher you raise the temperature, the faster they die.

Yeasts are also fungi, but they cause fermentation. Some are purposefully added to foods (think beer and bread). Others will make you pucker, as they sour foods in a not-so-appetizing way. They flourish at the same temperatures as molds and can be destroyed the same way.

Bacteria are what most people get worried about when canning comes to mind. Not only do some types thrive in temperatures that would normally wipe out molds and yeasts, certain kinds that thrive in specific types of food can cause paralysis and death (think *Costridium botulinum*, the bacterium that produces the botulism toxin).

The trick here is to know what food you're preserving and how to protect it from different bacteria types. Some germs, like the fragile *Salmonellae*, can be killed at a mere 140 °F as long as they are kept at that temperature for enough time. To protect against the botulism nerve toxin, conversely, you can either create an environment in which the bacteria cannot survive (highly acidic) or you have to heat the food to 240 °F (for which you need a pressure canner) for a certain amount of time.

Canning

Can I CAN without fear of Botulism?

Absolutely, YES!

Most people don't realize that it's easy to can without any fear of the botulism toxin—as long as you know which canning technique is right for the type of food you are canning. All *this* comes down to is a question of acidity.

High-Acid versus Low-Acid Canning

Clostridium botulinum, the bacterium that produces the botulism toxin, cannot survive in foods with a pH of 4.5 or lower. Some examples of these high acid foods are blackberries, peaches, and apples. You can also make food high acid by adding what? More acid! (think pickles).

Thus, canning comes down to knowing the acidity of your recipe:

If your food is **high acid** (or you have made it high-acid by adding something like vinegar), you can process it in a **water-bath canner**. In this system you submerge the food, inside of jars, in boiling water for a prescribed amount of time. This heating process will get rid of the other possible spoiling elements (enzymes, molds, yeasts, and the types of bacteria) and also seals the jar so that none of these spoilers can sneak in later. You don't need to heat the jar hot enough to kill *Clostridium botulinum* because it cannot live in the acidic environment of low pH foods.

If your food is **low acid**, then you need to heat it hot enough to kill the *Clostridium botulinum* bacteria. Low acid foods include vegetables without added vinegar, meat, and fish, just to name a few. The only way to get these foods to the temperature that kills these bacteria (240 °F, hotter than boiling) is with a special piece of canning equipment called a **pressure-canner**. Most canners say it's a good idea to become an expert water-bath canner before jumping in to using a pressure-canner, simply because it is an expensive piece of equipment that requires a bit of special maintenance. For that reason, we'll just look at water-bath canning in this guide. Check out the Resources section for some great books that can tell you all you need to know about how to choose a pressure-canner, use it, and most importantly, keep it working safely.

To find the pH of common foods, go to http://vm.cfsan.fda.gov, click on "Acidified and Low Acid Canned Foods," and then go to "Approximate pH of Foods and Food Products."

How Common is Botulism, and What Does it Do to You?

According to Patricia Telesco and Jeanne P. Maack in *The Everything Canning and Preserving Book*:

> In the United States, an average of 110 cases of botulism are reported each year. Of these, approximately 25 percent are food-borne, 72 percent are infant botulism, and the rest are wound botulism. Outbreaks of food-borne botulism involving two or more persons occur in most years and are usually caused by eating contaminated home-canned foods. (p. 22)

Botulism is a severe medical emergency that can cause paralysis and, commonly, death. That's why it's important to follow a few basic guidelines for avoiding the botulism risk.

How to Avoid the Botulism Risk:

Always follow a recipe!

All sorts of ingredients can change the pH of food, so you don't want to accidentally add one to your low-acid applesauce and end up with a concoction that is no longer safe to process in a water-bath canner. If a recipe calls for vinegar, that exact amount is there for a reason—to make the product a safe pH. Most tomato recipes, for example, call for added vinegar or citric acid because tomato pH is extremely variable and depends on variety and ripeness. Thus, be very suspicious if a tomato recipe doesn't call for these things! On that note...

Get your recipe from a reputable source!

All of the books listed at the end of this section are great resources. The Cooperative Extension offices of state universities are also great places to check out canning recipes. You know these recipes are safe because the pH of the produce has been tested in a lab setting. Though it might be tempting to try your great-great-grandmother's tomato-sauce recipe, compare it to some modern ones first, because in her time they didn't measure pH levels. Also be sure to check out up-to-date recipe sources, because guidelines for the correct boiling times on jars have changed numerous times.

Size up your jar—and boil it right!

Boiling times vary from recipe to recipe based on the size jar you are using and the food that you are canning. Eugenia Bone provides this reasoning, drawn directly from her book *Well-Preserved*:

> Different foods have different densities, which affects how long it takes for the heat to penetrate the food thoroughly and subsequently kill the spoilers and create a vacuum in the jar.

> The length of time needed to process a food also depends on the acidity (natural or added) of the food you are canning. That's because the pH, or acidity, of a food affects the ability of spoilers to thrive: the higher the acid content of the food, the less boiling time needed to kill spoilers.

Another factor in judging how long a product must boil is how large a jar you are processing. For example, it takes longer for the heat to reach temperature in the center of the food in a quart jar than a pint jar.

Don't assume a Peach is the same as a Nectarine!

Some fruits and vegetables may seem alike, but actually have different pH levels or different densities. Thus, they may require different additives or processing times. Peaches and nectarines are one example. An even more deceptive one is pears and Asian pears—the second of which is actually low acid and needs a pressure-canning process to be safe!

Water-Bath Canning

So now that you know the important safety background on canning, let's look at how to do it!

THE TOOLS OF THE TRADE:

Canning jars (Ball and Kerr are common brands) that use screw-on bands and lids.

Canning bands, either normal or wide-mouth, that fit your jars. Band can be re-used until they become too rusty or misshapen to tighten correctly onto jars.

Canning lids (special metal disks encircled by a rubberized flange on the inside). *Canning lids cannot be re-used after being processed,* as they will not seal correctly. Thus, you will need to purchase new ones every time you can.

A canner. This can be a large pot retro-fitted with a rack in the bottom (so the jars don't rattle and break), or a special canning pot that you pick up at a consignment store or hardware store. Nearly any pot will work—as long as it is deep enough to cover your jars by **at least two inches of water** (this space is key when processing jars because you want the entire jar to reach boiling temperature for the prescribed length of time) and to leave enough space above the water level so that the boiling water doesn't explode all over you and your stove.

A jar-lifter. Trust me—you want one! Otherwise, it is very tricky to lift steaming, slippery jars out of a roiling boil and carry them away to safety. They only cost a few dollars and will make your canning experience much more fun.

A lid-wand. This handy little tool helps you lift your lids and place them on jars without touching them—a nice way to reduce germ problems while canning.

You'll also want an assortment of **spoons, some oven mitts, a timer**, and probably a **kitchen scale** (helpful to get the recipes right).

The basic steps of water-bath canning are:

1. Prepare the food that you want to preserve.

2. Sterilize your canning jars (see below).

3. Pack the food into the jars and wipe off the rims (see below for directions on packing safely).

4. Place canning lids on the jars and gently tighten on the rims (only as tight as you can get with your fingertips—don't use your palms), placing jars into the pot of boiling water as soon as they are filled and covered.

5. Process the jars in boiling water for the prescribed time, adding additional minutes per these guidelines—www.ext.colostate.edu/pubs/foodnut/p41. html#can—if you decide to can in a location higher than 1,000 feet above sea level (because altitude affects the temperature at which water boils).

6. Remove the jars from the boiling water and set them somewhere to cool for 6 to 8 hours (when lifting them out of the water, keep the jars completely upright and do not tip off the water that will settle on top of the lids, as doing so could disturb the seal).

7. Check to make sure the jars are sealed. This is easy to tell because the lid will be taut and pulled down into the jar—it should not click or bounce when you press on it.

8. Remove the bands and make sure you can lift the jars by their sealed lids.

9. Store the jars without their rims in a cool, dark place (without the rims, you will easily see if a seal goes faulty) for up to a year. The ideal temperature range for safe storage is 50-70°F, and darkness is important if you don't want the sun to bleach the product.

    If you want to move jars, mail them, or give them as gifts, just screw the bands back on to protect the lid seals.

Sterilization

JARS:

To sterilize jars, process them in your canner for at least ten minutes. Because you want your jars to be hot when you fill them, leave them in boiling water in your canner until you are ready to pack them with your product. Then, take out one jar, pack it, screw it closed, and place it back in the boiling water immediately, before moving on to the next jar. This will mean that some jars process a little bit longer than others, but this process helps to make the canning safer. Some people choose to sterilize jars in their dishwasher (some models have special settings for this). If you choose this method, don't open the dishwasher until you are ready to fill the jars.

BANDS:

Wash in warm, soapy water, then sterilize in boiling water along with the jars.

LIDS:

Don't boil the lids because it can ruin the rubberized flange. Instead, right before placing them on your jars, simmer the lids in a small pan of water to soften the flange, which aids in the sealing process.

How to Pack the Sterilized Jars

Jars should be packed with produce to the specific jar-level that your recipe specifies. A recipe will usually call for a ½" or ¼" **headspace**, which is the amount of space between the top level of the food and the top of the jar. From the top of the jar to the bottom of the screw divots is ½". Thus, halve this if you need to leave a ¼" headspace. **It is important to follow this specification precisely.** Leaving too much headspace can cause pressure to build up inside the jar and crack the glass. It can also cause a seal failure. Conversely, leaving too little headspace might cause some food to be forced out under the lid when it expands during processing, also ruining the seal.

For some really excellent visuals to show you what this process looks like, see the Pressure Canning page on Virginia Tech's Cooperative Extension site, at:

http://pubs.ext.vt.edu/348/348-585/348-585.html

Once jars are filled, it is important to **remove all air bubbles.** According to the *Ball Blue Book of Preserving:*

> This can be done by placing a nonmetallic spatula inside the jar between the food and the side of the jar. Press spatula back against food to release trapped air. Repeat several times around the inside of the jar. Do not use metal knives or other metal utensils since they can scratch the glass and result in jar breakage. Even though air bubbles may not be visible, they can be trapped between pieces of food and must be removed (p. 11).

Recipes!

One of the best things for a new canner to experiment with is apple sauce, because it's nearly impossible to get wrong and it requires very few ingredients. Apples are also high-acid, so there is no risk of botulism poisoning.

Apple Sauce

+ 2 ½ to 3 ½ pounds apples per quart
+ Water
+ Sugar (optional)
+ Cinnamon, Nutmeg, Allspice (optional, to taste)

Wash apples. Core, peel (optional), and slice. Place in large saucepan with enough water to prevent sticking and cook until soft. Purée with a food processor or food mill, if a fine texture is desired, and return to saucepot. Otherwise, mash with a spoon or potato masher to remove clumps. Add ¼ cup sugar for each pound of apples, if desired, but sugar is usually not necessary. Bring applesauce to boiling (212 °F), stirring frequently to prevent sticking. Keep mixture at a boil while filling hot, sterilized jars. Leave a ½-inch headspace. Remove air bubbles (see above). Correctly place lids and rims. Process pints and quarts for 20 minutes in a boiling-water canner.

Processing directions adapted from Ball Blue Book of Preserving.

Berry Jam   *(Recipe adapted from Ball Blue Book of Preserving.)*

Blackberry, Blueberry, Boysenberry, Dewberry, Gooseberry, Loganberry, Raspberry, and Youngberry all make excellent jams, and this recipe works for each.

Yield: about 3 pints

- 9 cups crushed berries
- 6 cups sugar or equivalent sweetener (optional)

Combine berries and sugar in a large saucepot. Sweetener quantity may be safely varied according to personal taste. Bring slowly to a boil, stirring until sugar dissolves. Cook rapidly to gelling point. As mixture thickens, stir frequently to prevent sticking. Remove from heat. Skim foam if necessary. Ladle hot jam into jars, leaving ¼-inch headspace. Adjust two-piece caps. Process 15 minutes in a boiling-water canner.

Note: If seedless jam is preferred, crushed berries may be heated until soft and pressed through a sieve or food mill; measure pulp and proceed as above.

Frequently Asked Questions

Isn't canning a lot of work?

A lot of people have the impression that canning involves hours of heavy lifting and sweat in a steamy, 80 °F kitchen when the beach would be so much more fun… Some of this is true. Canning does take a lot of hours and it can get pretty hot. However, in a pinch, you can make it a lot more pleasant:

Can in small batches. Diversity can be a lot more fun than quantity. Buy or harvest small batches at a time, and set aside four hours. That's really all you need!

If canning in the heat of summer is too intimidating, freeze summer's bounty and **can at your leisure through the fall, winter, and spring.** Berries are easy to freeze (see the section on Freezing) and can be canned into jams in small batches. Freezing also allows you to experiment with combinations of produce that don't ripen during the same season (just be sure to follow a recipe or only mix fruits that have the same processing time and canning specifications).

Throw a canning party! Instead of hanging out with friends and just talking, have a lot to show for the time you spend together! You can all bring different produce and then do an exchange at the end to have even more delicious products stored away for the cold winter months.

Can I change the amount of sugar called for in a recipe, or omit it entirely?

Definitely. Sugar does not influence pH, so feel free to vary the amount according to personal preference. You can also substitute sugar with Splenda®, fruit juice, or honey. Official recommendations advise not substituting more than ½ of the sugar called for with honey. However, if you like the taste of honey and don't mind a slightly runnier or soggier product, you can substitute it entirely.

Do I have to use pectin when making jams and jellies?

Pectin is by no means necessary, and omitting it will not affect the safety of the recipe. Most people add pectin because it creates a more solid jam and makes the fruit stretch farther. This is because when you don't use pectin, you have to cook the fruit a lot longer to make it thicken. As this involves evaporating out the fruit's natural water content, in the end, you will have less jam left in the bottom of your pot when you don't use pectin. However, the taste of the jam should not be any different.

I don't want to buy pectin—can I make it myself?

Yes! Pectin occurs naturally in most fruit, but some, like apples and crab apples, have very high concentrations of this natural thickener. You can boil these fruits down to create your own pectin solution and add it to fruits that don't have enough natural pectin to thicken satisfactorily. The following website provides recipes and directions:

www.motherearthnews.com/Real-Food/1980-05-01/Make-Your-Own-Pectin.aspx

Pickling

Pickles are one of the oldest forms of food preservation. The number of different pickling techniques reflects this long history. It is impossible to do justice to this fine art here, so if you are interested in exploring the full diversity of pickling options, the book *The Joy of Pickling* is a must. Here you can read more about brining, relishes, quick pickles, chutneys, and how to pickle just about everything.

If you've never pickled before, however, and just want to give it a try (and get a delicious product on the first try), fresh-packed Dill Pickles are a wonderful place to begin. They do not require brining and can either be left in the refrigerator a few weeks to develop full flavor before eating, or canned for longer storage. Before beginning, this is the least you need to know:

PICKLING SALT: This is fine, pure granulated salt. You can usually buy four-pound boxes labeled "Canning and Pickling Salt" at most supermarkets. Kosher salt is also okay to use, but you need to use one and a half to two times as much to compensate for the larger salt crystals.

VINEGAR: Cider vinegar is considered the supreme pickling vinegar (beware of fake apple cider-flavored vinegar) but distilled white vinegar works great too. Just make sure that the vinegar you use is at least 5 percent acidity—necessary for maintaining a pH level at which harmful bacteria cannot survive.

PICKLING SPICES: You can buy packages of pickling spices at the grocery store, but it is also easy to make your own. *The Joy of Pickling* recommends the following mixture, which makes ½ cup. It calls for un-ground spices, though ground ones can be used. In this case, you may wish to wrap them in a piece of cloth to avoid muddying the pickle-solution.

+ One 4-inch cinnamon stick, broken into small pieces
+ 6 Mediterranean bay leaves, torn into small pieces
+ 6 small dried hot peppers, such as *japonés* or *de arból*, cut into small pieces
+ 1 tablespoon whole black peppercorns
+ 1 tablespoon whole yellow mustard seeds

- 2 teaspoons whole allspice berries
- 1 teaspoon whole cloves
- 2 teaspoons whole coriander seeds
- ½ teaspoon blade (unground) mace
- 1 tablespoon dill seeds

Now you're ready to make pickles! Here is a good recipe, adapted from the *Ball Blue Book of Preserving*:

DILL PICKLES

Yield: about 7 pints or 3 quarts

- 8 pounds 4- to 6- inch cucumbers, cut lengthwise into halves
- ¾ cup sugar
- ½ cup canning salt
- 1 quart vinegar
- 1 quart water
- 3 tablespoons mixed pickling spices
- Green or dry dill (1 head per jar)

Wash cucumbers, scrubbing well to remove dirt. Place sugar, salt, vinegar and water in a large saucepot. Add spices (in a spice bag if desired) and simmer 15 minutes. Pack cucumbers into hot, sterilized jars, leaving ¼-inch headspace. Place one head of dill in each jar. Ladle the hot vinegar solution over the cucumbers, leaving a ¼-inch headspace. Remove air bubbles using a non-metallic spatula. Adjust two-piece caps. Process pints and quarts 15 minutes in a boiling-water canner.

Recipe Variation: For Kosher-Style Pickles add to each jar: 1 Bay leaf, 1 clove garlic, 1 piece hot red pepper and ½ teaspoon mustard seed. Process as recommended above.

195

Freezing

Freezing is another great way to preserve summer and autumn's bounty to enjoy year-round. Pretty much everything can be frozen successfully except for eggs in the shell, cream sauces, mayonnaise, milk, and precooked meat (which becomes very dry).

Most people don't freeze more frequently simply because they don't realize how easy it can be! For example, if you go raspberry picking, all you need to do is spread the berries out on cookie trays in the freezer, let them set, and then shovel them into freezer bags. You can even wait to wash them until you want to use them! If you have a garden and don't know what to do with all your extra zucchinis, wash and slice them, blanch them for 3 minutes, and throw them in a freezer bag. They'll be delightful for zucchini bread in the winter. Or, in the fall, roast pumpkins in your oven, scoop out and puree the innards, pour them into a bag, and enjoy pumpkin pie, bread, and cookies even into the spring and summer.

It's hard to mess up freezing food, but a few simple tips can make you more satisfied with the end product.

Prepare the food item according to the following directions to preserve the taste, quality, and color. While blanching is not *necessary*, it stops the enzyme action that contributes to the slow deterioration of the product even while frozen.

Fruits

Freezing fruits in syrups protects them from the action of enzymes that will degrade the color and general aesthetics of the fruit. Depending on how you intend to use the product, this may not be important (for example, in making jams, smoothies, or covered pies). If you do wish to freeze fruits in syrup, Virginia Cooperative Extension recommends the following ratios of sugar to water:

Syrup type	*Light*	*Medium*	*Heavy*
Sugar	1 cup	1 3/4 cups	2 3/4 cups
Water	4 cups	4 cups	4 cups
Syrup yield	4 1/2 cups	5 cups	5 1/3 cups

VEGETABLES

For freezing vegetables, the Cooperative Extension Service at New Mexico State University provides a very helpful table, revised by Martha Archuleta, Food & Nutrition Specialist, and accessible on-line with instructions at http://aces.nmsu.edu/pubs/_e/e-320.pdf.

To blanch vegetables: Immerse the prepared vegetables in boiling water for the prescribed length of time. Remove and immediately submerse in an ice or cold-water bath (to preserve color). When cool, package for freezing.

GENERAL FREEZING TIPS

Freeze as quickly as possible. To minimize the formation of ice crystals, you may want to put your freezer on a quick-freeze cycle because the faster the food freezes, the fewer ice crystals will form. Otherwise, just try to put the food in the coldest part of your freezer when you first introduce it.

Freeze your food in bags and containers that are specifically designed for freezing. Though glass works too, be sure to leave extra space for food expansion and be careful when removing the jar as it will become slippery.

Package your food in easily-to-access quantities. If you are putting multiple servings in one bag, separate them with pieces of tin foil or cut-up plastic bags (try not to buy new products for this; just use wasted plastic and foil from packaging around your house).

If freezing liquids or sauces, you can freeze them in ice-cube trays and then transfer them to bags for quick-access later (that doesn't involve defrosting the entire container). This works great for pesto, salsas, and juices.

Bananas and other larger fruits can be frozen in sliced pieces to be easily added to smoothies.

Safety Practices when Freezing Foods

Freezing food is safe and effective, as long as your freezer can maintain a constant 0° F (-18° C). It is just important to be safe when defrosting food that has been frozen. In *The Everything Canning and Preserving Book*, Telesco recommends the following tried-and-true ways to safely defrost your food (p. 36):

Leave the food in your refrigerator. This takes a while, but is the most energy-efficient method. It's wise to put some paper towels down or a platter underneath the item to catch any water or juices that run out during defrosting.

Put the food in a cold-water bath. Keep the item in the wrapper or container, and if need be, put it in an additional resealable bag for protection. It's recommended that you refresh the water every 30 minutes until the item is defrosted.

Use the defrost setting on your microwave. Microwave powers vary greatly from machine to machine, so watch carefully to make sure your food isn't being partially cooked because that can give your food a rubbery texture. As with the refrigerator, you will want something to gather any liquid that's released during the process for faster cleanup.

It is safe to re-freeze food as long as it has not completely thawed or reached room temperature.

Drying & Dehydrating

If the last sections on canning and freezing seemed too intimidating, time-consuming, or potentially expensive, drying food may be a more fitting form of preservation. Beyond the pure tastiness of dried pear rounds or tomato slices in the winter, drying food is 1) very inexpensive 2) requires little space for food storage and 3) does not require the monetary and environmental toll of maintaining a large freezer.

Though it is costly in the sense that two large boxes of fruit will dehydrate into two quart-bags of dried fruit, those two bags still contain the same amount of food. If you are interested in making large quantities of dried food on a small budget, the best technique is to grow your own fruits and vegetables, buy "seconds" produce at Farmers Markets, or glean wild fruits and vegetables (readily available around many cities).

Equipment

Depending on your available time, financial resources, and preference, numerous drying methods are possible:

SOLAR DEHYDRATOR—The best option, environmentally, is to dry food outside under the sun in a hot climate or, in cool places such as Seattle, in a solar dehydrator. Though temperature may be more variable and require more monitoring in this method, no unsustainable energy inputs are required. Check out the Homegrown Evolution Blog for pictures and links to sites that can teach you how to build your own: www.homegrownevolution.com/2008/10/build-solar-dehydrator.html.

FOOD DEHYDRATOR MACHINE—Investing in a dehydrating machine is probably one of the easiest ways to dry food quickly and satisfactorily. Though it requires electricity, it is much more efficient than drying in an oven and does a much better job because it maintains the ideal drying temperature and needed air circulation. Brand new, dehydrators range in cost from $35-60 dollars, however, used dehydrators are easy to find at garage sales and discount stores.

Gleaning *is the act of allocating and collecting a little extra harvest for those in need.*

For more on gleaning in Seattle, check out Lettuce Link's Community Fruit Tree Harvest, & the great work of City Fruit, at **www.cityfruit.org**

DRYING IN YOUR OVEN—If you don't rely heavily on your oven for other purposes, you can use it to dry food (plan to double the drying time necessary when using a machine). Set your oven to 140 °F (you may need to use an internal thermometer to monitor this temperature) and prop the door open 1-2 inches. Ideally, use a convection oven with a fan (though not necessary). Place the food inside on well-oiled cookie sheets or cake cooking trays. You may need to flip and turn the pieces every few hours to aid in uniform drying.

Preparing Food for Drying

- Slice/peel fruits and vegetables as you will want to eat them. If you like to eat the skins of the food item fresh, you can leave them on for drying, though they will become tough when dried.

- Cut fruits and vegetables into uniform sizes and thicknesses so that they will dry evenly. Rather than drying apples and pears in wedges, for example, peel, core, and slice the fruits into rounds of equal thickness.

- **If drying vegetables, steaming or blanching prior to drying is recommended to prevent toughening of the dried product over time.**

Drying Process

- Arrange food in chosen location for drying.

- For ideal drying that preserves the texture, color, and nutritional quality, **maintain the temperature between 130 and 140 °F.**

- Monitor foods frequently and remove when pliable and leathery, not hard. Dry fruits to about a 20 percent moisture content. This means that when cut in half, you should not be able to squeeze out any juice, and the fruit should not stick to itself when folded in half. Berries will rattle when fully dry. Vegetables should be dried to a 10 percent moisture content, at which time they will be brittle and crisp.

Fun Stuff

*There are so many fun options for drying foods. Check out **www.pickyourown.org** and others in the Further Resources section (next page) for all the details about making Fruit Leather, Sun-Dried Tomatoes, Beef Jerky, and more!*

After Drying

+ Allow foods to cool completely.

+ Vegetables can be packed immediately for storage in air-tight bags or jars.

+ Fruits should be 'conditioned' prior to storage to allow any remaining moisture to be distributed evenly through the fruit (this step may be omitted, but will increase the chance of molding). **To condition fruit:** place the dried pieces loosely in plastic or glass jars for 7-10 days, shaking frequently. If condensation appears, the fruit should be returned to the dehydrator for additional time. Once the conditioning period has ended, package the fruit for storage.

Storage

+ Store dried food in sealed containers in a cool, dry place.

+ Pack in small quantities because each time a package is exposed to the air, its shelf life and overall quality may decrease.

+ Dried fruit generally can be stored for about a year if kept at 60 °F, or for six-months at 80 °F. Dried vegetables have roughly half the shelf life of dried fruits.

Preserving in Oil, Curing, & Smoking

These are some other great techniques for preserving food, albeit a bit less common. If you're interested in learning more about these delicious options, Eugenia Bone's book *Well Preserved: Recipes and Techniques for Putting Up Small Batches of Seasonal Foods* is a great resource, full of anecdotal notes about the Italian kitchens of her grandparents' generation and the artichokes her "Zia Ada bathes in homemade vinegar, preserves in her cousin's oil, and stores on the shelf" (that she can never say no to despite her Zia Ada's outdated safety precautions).

FURTHER RESOURCES & WORKS CITED:

Ball Blue Book of Preserving.
> Perhaps the most definitive book on food preservation out there; a "canner's Bible" of sorts, with all the necessary basics and safety information, presented in a concise and accessible manner.

Bone, Eugenia. *Well-Preserved: Recipes and techniques for putting up small batches of seasonal foods.*
> This book is witty and fun to read. Be prepared to get hungry reading it. Bone provides a selection of unique, gourmet canning recipes, each with its own array of recipes about how to use the canned produce when you finally pop the lid.

www.canningusa.com. "A Simple Approach to Preserving Home-made Foods."

RECIPES, VIDEO TUTORIALS, ETC.

www.homecanning.com
> A great source for buying canning tools, also with good canning and freezing instructions, including an on-line tutorial.

www.pickyourown.org
> My personal favorite for on-line canning/preserving help and guidelines. Though less polished aesthetically, the site has a seemingly endless assortment of new food ideas to discover.

Telesco, Patricia and Jeanne P. Maack. *Everything Canning and Preserving Book: All you need to know to enjoy natural, healthy foods year round.*
> This is a great resource with how-to descriptions of all preserving techniques as well as recipes for condiments, marinades, broths, spice mixtures, jams, and flower products.

Ziedrich, Linda. *The Joy of Pickling: 250 Flavor-Packed Recipes for Vegetables and More from Garden or Market.*
> Everything you could ever want to know about pickling. Plus More. Seriously.

Laura Brady lives in and around Seattle where she grows food, plays music, teaches Spanish, and works towards becoming a Permaculture designer.

Notes From Your Own Preserving Projects....

Resources & Inspiration:
Taking Action in Your Community

The CAGJ Editors

We give credit to Pesticide Action Network North America and the US Food Sovereignty Alliance for many of these inspirations & ideas.

Learn More!

Find out how your local efforts can help grow food democracy at home while also contributing to the world-wide movement for food sovereignty.

- Community Alliance for Global Justice: www.seattleglobaljustice.org
- US Food Sovereignty Alliance: www.usfoodsovereigntyalliance.org
- Community to Community Development: www.foodjustice.org
- Food First Institute: www.foodfirst.org
- Food Chain Workers Alliance: www.foodchainworkers.org
- Food and Water Watch: www.foodandwaterwatch.org
- Grassroots International: www.grassrootsonline.org
- National Family Farm Coalition: www.nffc.net
- Pesticide Action Network North America: www.panna.org
- Why Hunger: www.whyhunger.org
- Community Food Security Coalition: www.foodsecurity.org
- Youth Food Bill of Rights: www.youthfoodbillofrights.com
- La Via Campesina: www.laviacampesina.org

Dig In!

- Support local farmers' markets, CSAs, farmer and community food justice organizations. Visit a farm, buy local, organic and fair trade foods or products from locally owned markets and stores.
- Get your hands dirty! Plant a garden at home or as a community.
- Cook and eat your own food together.

Spread the Word!

+ Organize an event with a local speaker, discussion, teach-in, or film night in your town.

    ...Or just invite a few people over to your house to talk about what you can do right now to grow the local foods movement in the U.S and strengthen local economies everywhere.

+ Host a potluck with food you or your friends grew and talk about what it takes to have healthy, green, fair and affordable food for all.

+ Get fliers for a current campaign and hand them out or leave stacks at stores and coffee-shops.

+ Follow campaigns and actions online and share them with friends.

+ Declare a GM-free week or GM free zone in your home/neighborhood.

+ Start a "Divest from Monsanto" campaign at your university.

+ Start a student club or local group to take action on the Farm Bill.

+ Have your organization join the US Food Sovereignty Alliance.

Start Building!

Change happens from the bottom up. Local governments, schools, and businesses have a powerful influence on our food system.

+ Start or participate in your local Food Policy Council (www.foodsecurity.org) to create better policies where you live,

+ Advocate for local Fresh Food Financing (www.thefoodtrust.org) to provide low-interest loans to local food businesses,

+ Get your city to adopt a Food Charter (www.noffn.org/charter),

+ Engage your local school district (www.farmtoschool.org), institution or company to purchase more fresh food direct from local farmers.

Take Action (and beet the system)

+ The US Food Sovereignty Alliance, Pesticide Action Network, Oakland Institute, National Sustainable Agriculture Coalition and others have action alerts to make it easy to stay updated on urgent issues, and find out what steps to take. Addresses are on the next page.

- www.usfoodsovereigntyalliance.org
- www.panna.org
- www.oaklandinstitute.org
- www.sustainableagriculture.net

- www.citizenstrade.org
- www.laviacampesina.org
- www.nffc.org
- www.ufw.org

- **Make your voice heard at local, city, county, state, federal, and international levels** to advocate for issues or policies that will create better ways to produce and eat our food at home, in schools, and in our communities.
- Make your voice heard at the farmland, feedlot, manufacturer, warehouse, store, market, head office, shareholder meeting, or board room level to advocate for policies and practices that create better ways to produce and eat our food.
- **Stand in solidarity when workers are struggling for fair treatment** anywhere along the food chain; march, strike, or boycott products depending on the campaign.
- **Support the human rights of women, indigenous peoples, and immigrants**—sometimes refugees of our globalized, industrialized food system and directly impacted by it.
- **Encourage the USDA & other bodies to protect small family farms** and end corporate domination and power over food production & distribution; support land reform and access to land.
- **Oppose so-called "free trade" agreements and policies** that undermine local economies and agriculture; **support fair, local economies.**
- Occupy the food system.
- **Recognize that everyone should be included** in production, control, and access to good food regardless of race, class, ethnicity, gender, sexual orientation, ability, religion, citizenship, or community; support actions, projects and policies that recognize the global right to food.
- **Volunteer** for one of the many organizations advocating for farmers and farm/food workers.
- **Act to prevent climate change & preserve natural resources.**
- **Support the seven principles of food sovereignty:**

  1. Food as A Basic Human Right
  2. Agrarian Reform
  3. Protect Natural Resources
  4. Reorganize Food Trade
  5. End the Globalization of Hunger
  6. Social Peace
  7. Democratic control of production and trade

Index of Authors & Artists

Index of Authors

About Raj Patel:

Dr Raj Patel is an award winning writer, academic and activist. Educated at Oxford University, the London School of Economics and Cornell University, he is currently a Visiting Scholar at UC Berkeley's Center for African Studies, an Honorary Research Fellow at the University of KwaZulu-Natal, in Durban, South Africa and an IATP Food and Community Fellow.

He is the author of the internationally acclaimed "*Stuffed and Starved: The Hidden Battle for the World Food System*," and the New York Times and international bestseller, "*The Value of Nothing*." He has co-authored "*Food Rebellions*" with Eric Holt-Gimenez and Annie Shattuck, and co-edited "*Promised Land*," with Peter Rosset and Michael Courville. His work on sustainability, food, and economics has been translated into over a dozen languages.